# COACHING THE INVISIBLE

How Top Coaches Use Neuroscience, Emotional, and Spiritual Intelligence to Drive Results

**Sandhya Mathur**

Coaching The Invisible



ISBN Paperback: 978-93-343-5340-2
ISBN Hardback: 978-93-343-5599-4

Book Cover Designed by Shivshanker Shenoy
Illustrations by Sanjiv Mathur
Credits: Photo by Hobi Photography

Published by:
Shivshanker Shenoy

Edition 1 Ver110825-1@2025

*This book is dedicated to:*
*My parents, grandparents, and teachers: my earliest coaches in life.*
*You saw me, understood me, and celebrated my uniqueness.*
*You nurtured not just my mind, but my heart and spirit*
*bringing forth the best in me, and shaping the foundation*
*for the person and coach I would become.*
*To the spiritual teachers who entered my life at just the*
*right moments, guiding me inward, upward, and forward.*
*Years ago, I dedicated my profession to kosen rufu,*
*the cause of happiness for others.*
*Coaching the Invisible is born of that same vow.*

# Praise for Coaching The Invisible

*"Coaching the Invisible"* invites us to expand the boundaries of what coaching can be. Sandhya Mathur's writing bridges emotional intelligence, spiritual depth, and neuroscience to illuminate the subtle forces that shape human transformation.

This book is more than a guide - it's a challenge to the reader to go beyond models and methods to listen more deeply, feel more fully, and coach with a reverence for the whole person.

- *Jayne Morrison, Regional Network Director, Six Seconds MEAI*

"Coaching the Invisible" is a luminous guide that transforms how we understand the human heart of change. By weaving together neuroscience, emotional intelligence and spiritual insights, Sandhya's masterpiece unveils the hidden currents that shape behavior and spark lasting transformation.

What sets this extraordinary book apart is its soulful depth when it offers tools that whisper to the root, not merely the symptoms. It's an essential read for coaches, managers, and change-makers who yearn to transcend surface-level solutions and create transformational shifts.

- *Jean-Francois Cousin, former Chairman, ICF Global Board; global executive and team coach*

"A rare book that bridges science and soul. 'Coaching the Invisible' speaks directly to leaders who know that building a successful organization and creating a legacy is as much about rewiring beliefs as refining strategy. *Coaching the Invisible* reframes leadership coaching as an act of transformation, not transaction. A must-read for anyone shaping teams and organizations for sustainable growth."

- *Ashok Swarup, Former MD Corporate Affairs, Citibank, India*

"If you want to lead teams with agility, resilience, and trust, read this book."

- *Rajiv Nayyar, COO Lightstorm Telecom Ventures*

"*Coaching the Invisible* is about what it takes to be curious about oneself and learn to be better at one's craft using coaching. What drew me to the book was the simple line- 'Coaching drives emotions in people. People drive performance'. While the book speaks to the 'how', the endearing part is about the 'why' for that is the starting point.

Coming from a celebrated coach and someone who is an expert in this field, the book is a treasure trove of gems waiting to be mined by the discerning reader. A must-read book. And a must-re-read book. Thank you, Sandhya, for penning this book."

- *SV Nathan, Chairman, Visara Partners*

"This book is a masterclass in unravelling the spirit and essence of human behavior while at the same time, gives you tool kits and models that help shape human growth..."

- *Poonam Kaul, Former VP Brand and Communications, Pepsico, & CMO, Apple India*

In a world of tactical, quick-fix learning models and AI guided instructions, this book reminds us that true growth is very personal and comes after rewiring from within." A must read for anyone in the pursuit of growth that is deep and lasts...

- *Kaushik Bellani, Former C-Suite Executive at Tech Majors- Wipro, HP, IBM and Cisco Systems Ex-Managing Director, McGraw Hill Education India & Saarc*

"In a world increasingly driven by artificial intelligence and automation, Coaching the Invisible by Sandhya Mathur arrives at a crucial moment, reminding us of the profound humanism at the core of leadership and transformation. This book is a powerful reflection on what it means to coach not just behaviors, but the invisible forces beneath—the beliefs, emotions, and presence that make us truly human.

I've had the privilege of knowing Sandhya for over a decade, and her influence on my own coaching journey has been profound. She has helped me bring shape and structure to the subtler dimensions of coaching, transforming intuition into frameworks that are both practical and powerful. I have also witnessed many others thrive under her mentorship, evolving into confident, reflective coaches who today lead successful coaching practices of their own.

When I came across her reference to the Triveni Sangam, it struck a deeply personal chord. I studied engineering in Allahabad, where the sacred confluence of the Ganga, Yamuna, and the invisible Saraswati has long stood as a metaphor for integration of clarity and emotion, of science and the unseen. This book embodies that very spirit. It brings together neuroscience, emotional intelligence, and spiritual awareness into a cohesive current that invites lasting transformation.

What makes this work truly exceptional is its universality. Whether you're mentoring a team in Tokyo, navigating a leadership shift in Toronto, driving change in New York, coaching a founder in São Paulo, or holding reflective space in Brisbane, Coaching the Invisible offers insights that are relevant across contexts, cultures, and conversations.

This is not just a guide for coaches. It is a resource for anyone committed to elevating human potential with empathy, intention, and wisdom. It is a book I will return to often, and one I am proud to endorse.

- *Madhivanan T A; Director, Microsoft Hyperscale Supply Chain, Americas East & LATAM, Microsoft*

I'm overwhelmed with all the authentic words of appreciation… and there's much more after the Conclusion. — *Sandhya*

# Acknowledgements

To my clients and mentees - you have been the silent inspiration behind every insight, every transformation captured in these pages. This book is not just mine; it is born from our shared experiences, conversations, and courageous journeys. *I am, because you are.*

To my family - to my daughters, Pallavi and Anjali, for your love, patience, and the light you bring into my life. You held space for me even in moments of absence while I poured myself into this work. To Ameya, for all the deep intellectual discussions that impacted my initial draft, And to Sanjiv, my husband, a brilliant coach himself who has stood beside me like an invisible pillar; steady, silent, and strong. I could not have made it here without your unwavering presence and support.

To my colleague and dear friend, Sunil Lala - thank you for believing in me from day one. Your belief gave me the courage to trust my own voice.

And finally, to the unseen and unsung heroes – those who run the background of my life with quiet efficiency, allowing me to immerse fully in my purpose. You are rarely named, but never unnoticed.

— *Sandhya*

# Foreword

When Sandhya Mathur invited me to review an early manuscript of *Coaching the Invisible*, I wasn't prepared for how deeply it would resonate in me. I expected wisdom; after all, Sandhya is a masterful coach and mentor, yet what I discovered is something far more profound… This book literally awakens.

*Coaching the Invisible* is a luminous guide that transforms how we understand the human heart of change. By weaving together neuroscience, emotional intelligence, and spiritual insight, Sandhya reveals the often-unseen forces that shape behavior, shift identity, and spark lasting transformation. The beauty of this work lies in its layered depth, it speaks to both the coach's mind and the coach's soul.

I still recall a conversation I had with Sandhya during a reflective webinar we co-hosted for the International Coaching Federation community. As we explored the question of what it truly means to hold space for another human being, her words struck a deep chord. Sandhya said, "*We are not fixing or leading—we are remembering, together.*" And there resides the essence of this book. It is a powerful reminder that the greatest transformations happen not when we push, but when we listen from a place freed of ego. When we coach from presence, not performance.

In my own journey as an executive and team coach, serving clients across 60 countries, and in my role as Chair of the ICF Global Board in 2019, what I have always witnessed is that the most impactful coaches are not necessarily the most articulate or analytical; they are the ones who coach with depth, presence, and humility. They honor the invisible forces that shape human potential. Sandhya's work stands tall in that tradition. And her book embodies the next frontier of coaching; where science meets soul.

What sets Coaching the Invisible apart is its reverence for what cannot be seen; the unspoken emotions, the energy beneath resistance, the quiet wisdom in a client's pause. Sandhya teaches us to honor those moments. Her tools are practical, of course, and they are also soulful invitations to go deeper.

To coaches, this book offers a roadmap to deepen presence and evoke transformation with subtlety, grace and effectiveness. For leaders, Sandhya's work is an opportunity to grow not just in skills, but in soul, and therefore become the kind of leader whose very presence creates safety, inspiration, insights, and long-lasting positive impact.

With her signature blend of Eastern wisdom and Western models, Sandhya holds space for coaches, leaders, and change-makers who yearn to move beyond surface-level fixes. She invites us all to coach with clarity, humility, and a profound respect for the mystery and potential of human growth.

I believe *Coaching the Invisible* is a gift to our profession. It brings language for what seasoned coaches know intuitively, but may struggle to articulate. And it lights up a clear path for coaches and leaders who are just beginning their journey, showing them how to build mastery from the inside out.

May you read this book not just with your mind, but with your deepest presence. And may it transform the way you meet every client and every team, as you approach every conversation with reverence for the invisible.

***By Jean-François Cousin, MCC – Global Executive & Team Coach, Keynote Speaker, Former Chair, ICF Global Board***

# Author's Note

I was born into a family where devotion and discourse went hand in hand. Morning prayers echoed through the house, and evenings were filled with books, reflections, and spirited conversations.

My parents and grandparents opened a portal to the unseen for me. In my earliest memories, there was a big, beautiful, glossy book called *The Kalyan*, filled with vibrant pictures and stories of divinity and spirituality. My Dadi would sit with me for hours, narrating stories from the book.

Looking at pictures of Lord Krishna's life or the Rasleela was my first introduction to spirituality. My Nana would also regale me with stories of myth and legend. That glossy book brought those stories vividly to life. It was a monthly subscription, and I would wait eagerly to see what each month's stories would be.

My paternal grandmother's unconditional faith and my maternal grandfather's rational precision and wisdom gave me twin lenses through which I now see the world: reverence and inquiry. My parents nurtured this path as well, encouraging my explorations and offering insights of their own that deepened my understanding. My father, an engineer, nurtured in me a love for scientific enquiry; a curiosity that, over time, grew into a longing to bridge the seen and the unseen.

What truly set my journey as a coach in motion, what ignited my purpose, was a conversation I had with my mother at the age of ten. She told me there is a *Gyaan Marg* and a *Mukti Marg*. These are both paths toward liberation (*Mukti*) in Hinduism, but they differ in approach. *Gyaan Marg*, or the path of knowledge, emphasizes self-realization through intellectual understanding and discernment. *Mukti Marg*, or the path of liberation, is a broader term encompassing various approaches like *Bhakti* (devotion), *Karma* (action), and *Raja* (royal) yoga, all aimed at ultimate freedom. I remember drinking in her words. After thinking deeply, I asked her,

*"Why must we choose? Can't we follow both?"*

In many ways, that question became the trajectory of my life. A well-informed blend of spiritual reflection, intellectual questioning and emotional attunement.

Even as a child, I carried a quiet awareness of how things made me feel - what drew me, what unsettled me, what felt right. I sensed what felt alive or off long before I had the words for it. I couldn't always name those emotions, but I could feel them like colors just beneath the surface.

Each "why" became a doorway, a path inward, opening to layers of thought, feeling, and something even deeper. I found myself in soul-searching conversations with myself and with all the teachers the cosmic vastness sent my way.

At eleven, I entered a nationwide essay competition. The topic — *Science and Spirituality* —was given on the spot. I wrote from instinct and placed third nationally. That spark never left me. In the years that followed, I found myself drawn to the chakra system and fascinated by its resonance with quantum physics. The questions I asked were not just intellectual; they were deeply personal. My grandfather, a quiet scholar, often invited me to sit beside him as he translated Sanskrit verses into English. I was about twenty then, a young adult, but those moments felt sacred. I learned to listen, not just to the words, but to the silences in between. Not just for meaning, but for essence.

That early immersion in language, reflection, and spirituality quietly shaped me: a seeker, a coach, a translator of the invisible.

The greatest lesson Eastern philosophy keeps whispering is simple yet seismic: I change, and the environment changes. True transformation begins within. It is never about forcing the world or another person to bend to our will. Coaching honors this principle. It is, to me, a structured path into practical spirituality, a disciplined way of drawing forth the best potential already stirring inside every individual.

This book is an offering born of that lineage. It weaves emotional intelligence, spiritual insight, and the science of transformation into a single current. Wherever you are in your life, this book can be your catalyst. Use it as a bridge between the practical and spiritual, use it to engage your intellect AND intuition, and most importantly, use it as a kindling for your questions, a workbook for your instincts and a friend to your deepest feelings.

If you are a coach, a leader, or a fellow seeker, may these words meet you where you are and gently guide you inward. May it serve as a companion on your own journey into presence, into essence, into the space where true change begins.

# Contents

# Introduction: Coaching Beyond the Surface

### *Coaching the Invisible: How Top Coaches Use EQ, SQ and Neuroscience to Drive Results*

I didn't come into coaching from the world of processes and performance. When I first entered the world of coaching, I found myself stepping into what looked like a well-organized, beautifully designed house. The frameworks were clear. The models were structured. The conversations followed a predictable rhythm: goals, actions, accountability. It was neat. Professional. Effective.

And yet, I often felt like we were only ever repainting the walls and making the space look fresh, without really changing the foundation.

You see, I came into coaching from a very different place, one shaped by spiritual inquiry, emotional depth, and the subtle wisdom of the inner world. I had long learned to sit with discomfort, to listen to what was unspoken, and to trust that transformation often begins in silence, not in strategy.

So, while many around me leaned heavily into process-driven coaching that was clean, tidy, and goal-oriented, I felt something was missing. Not wrong, just incomplete.

What I was seeking, and what I eventually began to build, was a way to coach beyond the surface. To go beneath the behaviors and beliefs, down into the roots. To help clients not just solve problems, but to understand the stories behind them. And most importantly, to integrate the science of change with the soul of transformation.

> *"Emotions drive people. People drive performance."*
> – Six Seconds

This deceptively simple truth has echoed through every meaningful coaching conversation I've had. It was one of the first things I learned from my time with Six Seconds, one of the world's foremost organizations for emotional intelligence education, and it continues to be the most enduring.

Beneath every decision, behind every goal, within every resistance or breakthrough, there is an emotional driver—a need, a belief, a hope, a fear. And when we access that, we don't just help someone perform better, we help them come alive.

Coaching that focuses only on behavior or outcomes is like painting the walls of a house while ignoring the foundation. Sustainable transformation requires us to go deeper. It invites us to shift from surface-level change to inner alignment: from doing to being, from fixing to feeling.

This book is an invitation to coach beyond the visible, to work with the invisible forces that shape human experience: emotions, identity, values, patterns, intuition, presence.

It brings together the emotional intelligence framework I absorbed through Six Seconds, the spiritual principles that have shaped my worldview, and insights from neuroscience that confirm what ancient wisdom has long known. We change not by force, but by awareness.

Coaching the invisible means returning to what truly drives people. If emotions are the fuel, then presence is the ignition. Together, they awaken movement from the inside out.

It's for the coach who loves structure and senses there's something deeper waiting to be touched.

It's for the practitioner who wants to go beyond performance goals and KPIs and into the real, raw, beautiful mess of human change.

It's for those who know that coaching is not just about progress; it's about presence.

My roots were grounded in something very different: spirituality, self-awareness, and emotional depth. I had spent years exploring inner transformation, understanding how emotions shape our experience, and how stillness often reveals more than words.

So, when I formally entered the world of coaching, I was excited. I thought, "This is where it will all come together." But what I found, at first, surprised me.

Coaching, as it was widely being practiced, was highly process-driven. Structured. Linear. Goal-focused. The models were neat, the competencies well-defined, the questions sharp and to the point. There was tremendous value in that, no doubt, but something felt missing.

Not because these models were flawed, but because they were only part of the story. Structure was the doorway, but what lay beyond was the terrain of transformation.

I noticed it myself. And I noticed it even more in the coaches I mentored.
They were sincere, skilled, and committed. But their sessions often stayed on the surface. There was a hesitance, almost a belief, that good coaching meant staying in the lane of process. That emotion was a distraction. That intuition was unreliable. That spirituality had no place in a professional conversation. And yet, I could sense the undercurrent. Clients were bringing their fears, their stuckness, their search for meaning.

Emotions were bubbling underneath goals. Values were whispering behind actions.
But these were often left untouched. Unacknowledged.
That's when I realized: I had to create space for something different.

## Coaching's Evolution: From Skills to Transformation

In the early years of my coaching, I tried to adapt. I followed the process. I applied the models. And yes, they worked, to a degree.

Clients achieved outcomes. Feedback was positive. But inside, I felt restricted. I knew that transformation didn't happen through technique alone. It happened in moments of deep connection. Moments when a client touches something within themselves they hadn't met before.

Gradually, I began integrating what I had always known: my spiritual grounding, my sensitivity to emotion, my intuitive knowing, with the structure of coaching. I didn't reject the process; I simply stopped letting it define the entire journey. And what I saw was astonishing.

When structure met presence, when goals were held with compassion, when emotion wasn't bypassed but honored, coaching became transformational.
My clients didn't just shift behavior; they shifted consciousness. They began to meet parts of themselves they had long ignored. And from that place, results came, with more alignment, joy, and sustainability.

I once coached a high-performing executive who couldn't name a single emotion beyond "frustrated." Beneath his goals sat grief. And beneath the grief was the longing to be heard, not just respected. It was only when we sat with the invisible that true movement became possible.

Coaching, I realized, wasn't just evolving. It was remembering something ancient. Something human.

Coaching has grown rapidly, from a skills-based, performance-focused intervention into a dynamic, human-centered journey of growth. The coaching of today is no longer just about guiding someone from Point A to Point B. It's about walking beside them while they discover who they truly are, what they believe, and how they wish to live and lead.

The coach is no longer just a guide with a map, but a mirror, a witness, and a safe place to explore the unknown.

## Coaching the Invisible: Beyond Techniques

So, what do I mean by coaching the invisible?

It's coaching the unspoken. The subtle. The essence behind the expression. It's tuning in to the client's energy as much as their words. It's the tremor of truth when they say, "I don't know why, but this really matters to me." It's holding space not just for the goal, but for the person behind the goal.

In my work as a mentor coach, I often see mentees rush to the next question, the next step.

They fear the silence. They want to *do*. And yet, the most powerful coaching often happens when we *be*, when we sit with what's emerging, when we don't rush to fix or guide, but allow the invisible to become visible in its own time.

This is not soft or indulgent work. It is deep work. It is the kind of coaching that creates sustainable change, because when a client sees themselves clearly, when they connect to what truly matters, action becomes natural. It flows from alignment, not pressure.

And this style of coaching, while intuitive, is also teachable when we embrace the full spectrum of human intelligence. There is a landscape beneath every coaching conversation. One that's unseen, but deeply felt. It's made of emotions, unconscious beliefs, lived experiences, energy, and presence. It's where the real work happens.

Techniques are like tools in a toolbox. Useful, yes. But transformation often happens not because we used the right tool, but because we knew when to put the tool down and simply be there. Curious, attuned, fully present.

I invite you to listen beyond the words, to sense what lies beneath the spoken, and to trust your own deeper knowledge as a coach.

## How EQ, SQ, and Neuroscience Shape the New Coaching Paradigm

Think of coaching as a tree:

- Neuroscience is the root system, grounding change in the biology of how the brain rewires thought patterns.
- Cognitive intelligence (IQ) forms the soil, providing analytical clarity, frameworks, and insights from structured reflection and assessments.
- Emotional intelligence (EQ) is the trunk, holding the weight of self-awareness, empathy, and connection.
- Spiritual intelligence (SQ) is the canopy, reaching toward meaning, purpose, and the wisdom of the whole self.

Together, they create a living system where transformation can truly take root. When we coach from this integrated space, where science supports soul and structure supports surrender, we begin to see shifts that last. Not just behavior change, but identity shift. Not just outcomes, but evolution.

Over time, I found language for the kind of coaching I had been practicing. It lived at the intersection of Emotional Intelligence (EQ), Spiritual Intelligence (SQ), and Neuroscience.

EQ helped me ground emotions not as distractions, but as vital information. It gave my clients a map to understand their inner world and relate more authentically with others. It taught me, as a coach, the power of empathy and emotional regulation in building trust and depth.

SQ gave voice to the intangible: the yearning for meaning, the values that anchor us, the quiet wisdom that knows before it explains. It isn't about religion. It's about awareness, purpose, and deep coherence. It helped my clients shift from ego-driven ambition to soul-aligned purpose.

And neuroscience provided the structure my logical mind needed. It explained why safety matters, why change feels hard, and how deep coaching literally rewires the brain. It validated the role of cognitive insight and gave form to the invisible. It bridged the world of science with the world of spirit.

Blending these three - EQ, SQ, and neuroscience - has helped me evolve a style that is structured yet soulful, grounded yet intuitive. A style that honors goals and metrics, but also honors stillness, reflection, and emergence.

## The Sacred Confluence: A New Way Forward

There is an ancient metaphor that perfectly mirrors this integration. In India, there is a sacred place known as the *Triveni Sangam*, the confluence of three rivers:

- the Ganga, symbolizing knowledge that flows across lifetimes;
- the Yamuna, embodying the emotional richness and learning of the present; and
- the Saraswati, the invisible, subterranean stream of higher wisdom that cannot be seen, only felt.

Just like the *Sangam*, transformational coaching flows from the convergence of three powerful intelligences: the neuroscientific, the emotional, and the spiritual.

This book is an invitation to that inner *Sangam*, to stand at that sacred confluence where grounded science meets emotional truth and invisible wisdom.

To coach not just with models, but with presence. To witness not just what the client wants to do, but who they are becoming.
Because when we coach the invisible, we don't just change lives - we awaken them.
This book reflects that journey.

It is an invitation to coaches, whether you are new to the path or have been walking it for years, to look again.
To go beyond the visible.
To trust what you feel.
To explore the inner landscape of your client with as much reverence as the outer.

Because when we coach the invisible, we awaken something profound, not just in the client, but in ourselves.

As you read this book, listen with your mind, and with your presence.

What invisible threads are waiting to be seen in your own practice?

# Part One

# The Science of Coaching – How the Brain Drives Change

Through part 1, we explore the invisible landscape of transformation: how coaching touches not just what we do, but who we are becoming. To move from theory to transformation, we must understand where this shift begins; not just in our stories or emotions, but deep within the brain's wiring.

To understand why coaching works so deeply, we must explore where change actually occurs; not just in feelings or habits, but in the architecture of the brain itself. This next chapter opens that doorway.

# Chapter 1: How Coaching Rewires the Brain

***"The mind, once stretched by a new idea, never returns to its original dimensions."*** - *Oliver Wendell Holmes Jr.*

As a coach, I've witnessed transformations that can't be seen but are deeply felt; changes in presence, in perspective, in peace. Over time, I realized those changes weren't just emotional. They were neurological.

Transformation through coaching doesn't just show up in behavior or performance, it begins deep within the brain. While coaching may look like a dialogue on the outside, internally it's a neurological process that influences our brain's architecture, particularly through a concept known as neuroplasticity.

Understanding how coaching affects the brain helps us become more intentional, compassionate, and effective as coaches. It shifts our focus from trying to fix behavior to creating conditions for lasting internal change.

At the heart of ethical coaching lies a delicate dance between emotion, cognition, and regulation. Neuroscience reveals that ethical decision-making isn't just a matter of values; it's deeply influenced by the interplay between the prefrontal cortex (responsible for reasoning and long-term thinking), the amygdala (which processes threat and emotional intensity), and the anterior cingulate cortex, which helps navigate moral conflict. When a coach cultivates presence and emotional regulation, they activate the neural circuits associated with empathy, fairness, and impulse control; creating the conditions for grounded, ethical choices even in ambiguity. This makes the coach's inner state not just a moral anchor, but a neurological foundation for boundary-sensitive, bias-aware, and conscious decision-making.

## The Brain and Neuroplasticity

*Like a path through a forest, the more we walk a thought, the clearer it becomes.*

Neuroplasticity refers to the brain's ability to reorganize itself by forming new neural connections throughout life. These changes occur in response to learning, experience, and even intentional thought and practice

In coaching, this is critical. Clients shift from habitual, often unconscious patterns of thought and action to more conscious, empowering ones.
When clients revisit and reframe limiting beliefs or practice new behaviors during coaching, they are engaging neural pathways that, with repetition and reinforcement, become more dominant. Hebb's Law, "neurons that fire together wire together", explains this process.

Reflection*: What repeated thoughts or beliefs might your client be reinforcing unconsciously?*

As new thoughts and actions are reinforced, older, less useful pathways are pruned - a process known as synaptic pruning.

## Coaching and Habitual Patterns

*Old habits are like grooves in a vinyl record, coaching helps lay down new tracks.*

Habits are governed by subcortical structures such as the basal ganglia. These structures help automate repeated behaviors, which is efficient for the brain but can also trap individuals in unhelpful patterns

Coaching interventions disrupt these automatic loops by bringing them to conscious awareness, engaging the prefrontal cortex (PFC) : the area responsible for executive function, decision-making, and self-regulation .

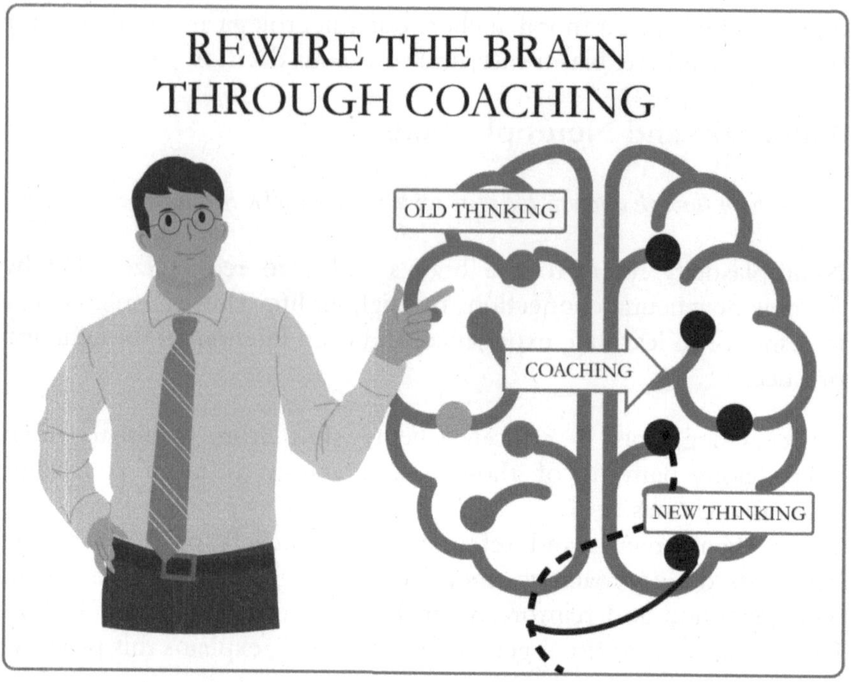


Repeated coaching conversations that focus on insight, reflection, and conscious action allow clients to develop new behavioral patterns. This helps shift neural activity from the reactive basal ganglia to the intentional and adaptive circuits of the PFC.

Coaching Tip: Help clients identify a habitual response and choose a new action, reinforcing it through repetition.

## The Role of the Prefrontal Cortex and the Amygdala

Think of the prefrontal cortex as the wise driver and the amygdala as the emergency brake; both essential, but not at the same time.

The PFC is central to reflective thinking, emotional regulation, and long-term planning. In contrast, the amygdala governs threat detection and emotional reactivity. Under stress, the amygdala activates the body's fight-flight-freeze response, reducing activity in the PFC, a phenomenon known as amygdala hijack.

Effective coaching creates a psychologically safe environment, helping down-regulate the amygdala and restore executive functioning in the PFC. This enables clients to reflect, access deeper insights, and make conscious choices rather than reactive ones.

Reflection: *In moments of emotional intensity, how can you help your client return to a state of calm awareness?*

Think of every human brain as a finely crafted grand piano. When one string is struck, sympathetic strings vibrate in resonance. Mirror neurons work like invisible tuning forks inside that piano: the moment you, as coach, strike the note of calm presence and genuine curiosity, your client's neural strings begin to vibrate at the same frequency. The resulting harmony quiets the amygdala's alarm bells and opens the melodic space of the prefrontal cortex for insight and creative problem-solving. In this way, *relationship literally becomes resonance*—and trust, empathy, and connection are the music that fills the room.

## Limiting Beliefs and Identity-Level Change

*Beliefs are like wallpaper you forgot you chose and coaching invites you to redecorate consciously.*

Core beliefs are stored in the brain's implicit memory systems, including the hippocampus and amygdala. These beliefs are often formed early and become unconscious patterns that shape identity and behavior (Kandel, 2007). Coaching brings these implicit patterns to light and helps rewire them through conscious reflection, emotional safety, and supportive action planning.

By enabling clients to name, question, and reframe their beliefs, coaches help initiate changes in both the structure and function of the brain. This process supports both unlearning and relearning at the identity level.

Coaching Tip: *When clients articulate a limiting belief, pause and ask: Who taught you that? Is it still true today?*

## Case Study: Rewiring a Leader's Identity

Name: Anand

Profile: CXO at a leading MNC

Consider a senior executive who came into coaching with the goal of improving delegation. Beneath this surface-level objective, however, lay a deeper narrative, one shaped by years of reinforcing a belief that "*asking for help is weakness.*"

This belief had become automatic, embedded in the neural pathways that governed his leadership behavior. Through consistent coaching sessions that focused on slowing down, building emotional safety, and inviting reflection, the client began to recognize the roots of this belief. As he engaged in small experiments, like expressing uncertainty in a team meeting or choosing to pause rather than react; his prefrontal cortex gained more access, and his habitual fear-based responses diminished. Over time, these repeated experiences created new neural associations: vulnerability became linked with authenticity, not threat.

This is neuroplasticity in action. What began as a conversation about performance became a process of rewiring identity.

## Co-Regulation and the Coach-Client Relationship

*A calm nervous system is contagious, like tuning forks, we attune to one another.*

The quality of the coach-client relationship also has neurological implications. Through presence, empathy, and attuned listening, coaches support co-regulation; a process where one nervous system helps another return to balance.

Mirror neurons, discovered in the premotor cortex, allow individuals to internalize the emotional states and intentions of others. A coach's calm presence can trigger similar calmness in the client's nervous system, opening up space for reflection and insight.

Reflection: *How might your energy, pace, and presence influence the client's nervous system?*

## Key Takeaways

- Neuroplasticity enables lasting change through new thought and behavior patterns.
- Coaching engages the prefrontal cortex and helps regulate emotional reactivity.
- Limiting beliefs can be surfaced and rewired through safe, reflective dialogue.
- The coach-client relationship supports nervous system regulation and insight.

*Pause here. Breathe. What in your own mental wiring might be ready for re-routing?*

The brain is the soil; coaching is the gardener's hand creating conditions for change.

Scientific research now confirms what many coaches have observed intuitively: coaching changes the brain. Through repeated reflection, emotional safety, and intentional practice, coaching supports neuroplasticity, disrupts limiting habits, and rewires beliefs—laying the neurological groundwork for lasting transformation.

## References

Chechik, G., Meilijson, I., & Ruppin, E. (1999). Neuronal regulation: a mechanism for synaptic pruning during brain maturation. Neural Computation, 11(8), 2061-2080.

Draganski, B., Gaser, C., Busch, V., Schuierer, G., Bogdahn, U., & May, A. (2004). Changes in grey matter induced by training. Nature, 427(6972), 311-312.

Goleman, D. (1995). Emotional Intelligence: Why It Can Matter More Than IQ. Bantam.

Graybiel, A. M. (2008). Habits, rituals, and the evaluative brain. Annual Review of Neuroscience, 31, 359-387.

Hebb, D. O. (1949). The Organization of Behavior. Wiley.

Kandel, E. R. (2007). In Search of Memory: The Emergence of a New Science of Mind. W. W. Norton.

LeDoux, J. E. (2000). Emotion circuits in the brain. Annual Review of Neuroscience, 23(1), 155-184.

Miller, E. K., & Cohen, J. D. (2001). An integrative theory of prefrontal cortex function. Annual Review of Neuroscience, 24(1), 167-202.

Pascual-Leone, A., Amedi, A., Fregni, F., & Merabet, L. B. (2005). The plastic human brain cortex. Annual Review of Neuroscience, 28, 377-401.

Porges, S. W. (2011). The Polyvagal Theory: Neurophysiological Foundations of Emotions, Attachment, Communication, and Self-regulation. Norton.

Rizzolatti, G., & Craighero, L. (2004). The mirror-neuron system. Annual Review of Neuroscience, 27, 169-192.

Siegel, D. J. (2012). The Developing Mind: How Relationships and the Brain Interact to Shape Who We Are. Guilford Press.

# Chapter 2: The Hidden Power of Words in Coaching

***"Language shapes the way we think, and determines what we can think about."*** - *Benjamin Lee Whorf*

If coaching is the art of rewiring the brain, then words are the invisible currents that spark that transformation. Every phrase spoken aloud, every silent mantra repeated in the mind, leaves a subtle mark on the neural landscape, like brushstrokes shaping the canvas of one's consciousness. Transformation does not arrive merely through insights. It begins, quietly and powerfully, with language.

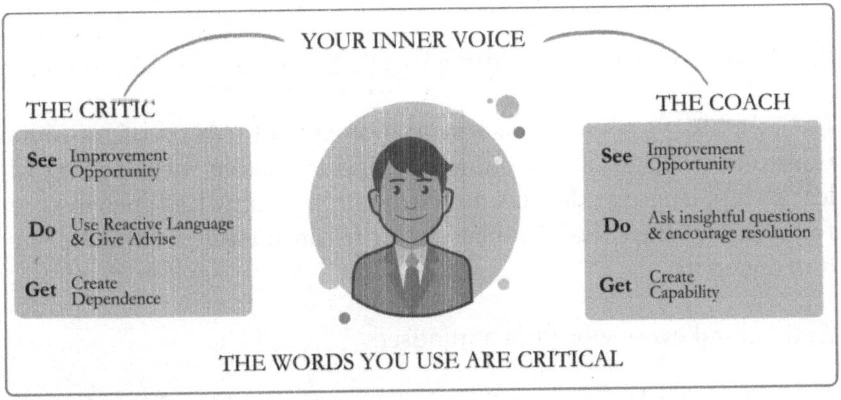


Imagine this: A leader stands before a boardroom. Heart racing. Thoughts spiraling. Two inner voices duel for control:

"You're out of your depth."
"You've trained for this moment. Breathe."

In milliseconds, the body obeys whichever sentence wins. Shoulders slump or square. Breath shortens or steadies. Words send biochemical instructions faster than conscious logic can keep pace.

Let us meet the sculptor behind the scenes: the hidden power of words.

## Architecture of Transformation

Picture a vaulted cathedral held aloft by four invisible pillars. Remove any one, and the ceiling collapses. Words operate the same way in coaching conversations, forming an unseen architecture that holds space for growth.

We often underestimate the influence of a single sentence. Yet the words we whisper to ourselves before stepping into uncertainty; "*I can handle this,*" "I belong here," "I know who I am" are not mere encouragement. They are catalysts. At a neurobiological level, they reconfigure internal chemistry. They shift their posture. They recalibrate possibilities.

Words are not just sounds strung together. They are carriers of energy.

Each phrase we speak, especially in moments of tension or transition, transmits emotion, intention, and relational charge. In coaching and leadership, language doesn't merely describe reality; it shapes it. It can forge safety, trust, and connection, or it can fracture confidence and dim creativity.

And behind every word lies a mindset.

A coach or leader's vocabulary is shaped by the lens through which they view the client and themselves. 'If I regard someone as capable, my language will be empowering. If I see them as fragile, my words may become tentative or corrective'. What we believe, we speak, and what we speak, we shape.

This is why embodying a coaching mindset; rooted in trust, presence, and nonjudgment is foundational. Mindset precedes method; it determines the language we choose, the pauses we allow, and the questions we ask.

Emotional intelligence is the silent architect of this expression. The more we cultivate self-awareness, the more conscious we become of the emotional charge beneath our words. The more we build social awareness, the more attuned we are to how language lands : opening a client's nervous system to insight and trust or closing it in defense. Language is not separate from presence; it is a reflection of it.

The energy behind our language; tone, tempo, and timing either opens or closes the doorway to transformation. As coaches and leaders, our task is not merely to choose words but to embody the consciousness that gives those words their power.

This Chapter Explores Four Core Ideas:

1. How self-talk sculpts the emotional brain
2. The alchemy of reframing through cognitive reappraisal
3. The neuroscience of transformational coaching questions
4. A lived example of leadership transformed by language

## The Silent Sculptor: Neuroscience of Self-Talk

The human brain is a relentless eavesdropper. Whether we speak aloud or think silently, it listens—and it believes us.

Self-directed speech, or "inner talk," activates the same neural pathways as external dialogue. The brain does not distinguish between the voice of another and the voice within. This means that the language we habitually use to describe ourselves, our situations, and our future becomes a script. Over time, it solidifies into a neural blueprint—guiding behavior, emotion, and belief.

Functional MRI studies show that inner dialogue lights up the medial prefrontal cortex (self-referential thought) and anterior cingulate cortex (error detection). Positive self-cueing also recruits the ventromedial prefrontal cortex, dampening amygdala reactivity and signaling safety through the vagus nerve; a Polyvagal win for calm focus. Mirror-neuron networks simultaneously notice the coach's language, meaning our clients literally "catch" our word patterns.

Consider the difference between two inner voices:

- "This always happens to me. I never get it right.
- "This is hard, but I'm learning every time."

The first entrenches limitation. The second opens a door. One tightens the nervous system; the other signals adaptability.

One study published in *Psychological Science* revealed that when individuals used their own name during inner dialogue—such as "Ananya, you've done this before"—they performed better under pressure. This subtle shift helps create psychological distance from reactive emotion and engages the brain's executive-functioning centers. In essence, the individual becomes their own coach.

Self-talk is not idle thought. It is instruction. It conditions emotional reactivity, resilience, and relational presence.

Coaches, therefore, serve as tuning forks; helping clients hear, shape, and ultimately reauthor their inner dialogue. We do not overwrite the voice. We help calibrate its frequency to resonate with courage, clarity, and choice.

## The Reframe: From Cracked Lens to Clear Vision

Imagine looking at life through a pair of smudged glasses. Everything appears distorted, heavy, and uncertain. Cognitive reappraisal; in coaching we call it "reframing", as the act of cleaning those lenses. It does not erase reality. It illuminates new angles of it.

When a client says, "I failed," the coach's work begins not in fixing the problem, but in exploring the meaning embedded in that word. What does failure signify? What assumptions ride within it? And what might emerge if the story shifted?

Reframing is not about offering a silver lining or negating pain. It is about restoring agency.

For instance:

- "I failed" becomes "I experimented."
- "They rejected me" becomes "They chose what was right for them, and I am still whole."
- "I'm not good at this" becomes "I'm in the middle of learning something important."

These are not mere linguistic tweaks. They are neurological interventions. Reframing engages the prefrontal cortex—the part of the brain responsible for reasoning and planning—and soothes the amygdala, the seat of emotional reactivity. In that moment, the client does not just see the world differently—they feel it differently. That shift in emotional tone makes new action possible.

*A useful framework:*

1. Notice the limiting narrative
2. Name the emotion it evokes
3. Narrate anew with a lens of growth or agency

Micro dialogue in action:

Client: "I failed again at setting boundaries."

Coach (softly): "What if we looked at this as information rather than failure? What is this moment teaching you?"
*(Pause… breath… shoulders drop.)*

Language, when reframed, becomes a tool of liberation. When language reframes perspective, questions become the catalysts that unlock it.

## Coaching Questions: Keys That Unlock the Mind

True coaching questions do not offer answers. They evoke them. They are keys that open locked rooms in the psyche—rooms where truths have been waiting to be remembered.

When a coach asks a well-crafted question, something lights up in the brain. Specifically, the prefrontal cortex is activated. This is where insight, integration, and creative problem-solving reside. When this part of the brain is engaged, clients move out of reactive survival and into possibility.

A SEE design lens helps craft catalytic questions:

- S – Struggle: Surface the edge or tension
- E – Emotion: Name the felt sense underneath
- E – Emergence: Invite what new awareness wants to arise

The most powerful questions have three qualities:

- Expansive: "What else might be true?"
- Heart-led: "What do you need in order to move forward with courage?"
- Visionary: "What would your future-self want you to know right now?"

Questions are not neutral. They carry tone, tempo, and subtext. A coach's question should not just provoke thought—it should invite presence.

Six gateways of inquiry:

- What – invites observation and clarity
- Why – touches meaning and motivation
- Who – explores identity and relationship
- How – engages process and agency
- When – locates timing and readiness
- Where – brings somatic and contextual awareness

Neuro Nugget: Using a client's first name in a question ("Ann, what do you sense here?") boosts executive-function engagement and calms the threat response by creating gentle psychological distance.

Coach's Cue: If a client is stuck in a story, switch to *Where* questions ("Where do you feel that in your body?"). Somatic focus often unlocks fresh data.

The simplest questions, asked with clean intent, can relocate a client from the landscape of limitation to the horizon of possibility.

## Language Across Cultures: A Deeper Reflection

Words carry history. They hold the weight of rituals, roles, resistances. A phrase that inspires in one culture may alienate in another. A metaphor that evokes growth in one language might feel disconnected or even disrespectful in another. As global coaches, we work not only with language but with lineage.

We honor linguistic diversity by:

- Checking metaphors for cultural fit
- Inviting clients to translate insights into their mother tongue
- Holding curiosity when language lands flat
- Being willing to repair or revise language in real time

Language is not universal—it is relational. Sensitivity isn't a side note. It's central to transformational work.

## Case Study: The Language of Leadership

Name: Priya

Profile: Senior Creative Leader

Let us meet Priya, a senior leader who came into coaching carrying the quiet weight of imposter syndrome. Her language was revealing:

- "I'm just lucky to be here."
- "I'm not strategic."
- "Soon they'll realize I'm not as capable as they think."

Priya once described herself as "a graceful swan paddling furiously beneath the surface." That metaphor became our entry point.

Through our work together, we unearthed those grooves, not to shame them, but to rewire them. Her new narratives emerged as grounded recognitions:

- "I've earned my place through consistent effort."
- "My intuition is a form of strategic thinking."
- "I lead by learning, not by knowing it all."

One afternoon, during a high-stakes meeting, Priya paused mid-sentence and said, "Let me rephrase that. I do bring strategic value. I just define it differently." The room shifted. Her voice landed differently. The energy realigned.

Over time, her internal dialogue softened. Her external communication strengthened.

## Key Takeaways

- Words are not passive descriptors; they are active builders of perception
- Self-talk is a neurological script—what we repeat, we reinforce
- Reframing is not positive spin—it is cognitive freedom
- Coaching questions are not inquiries—they are catalysts for neurobiological change
- Transformation often begins with shifting a single sentence

## Reflective Prompt for Coaches

What phrase do you repeat to yourself before stepping into a challenge?

How might a single word upgrade shift your chemistry, posture, and possibility today?

## Reflection

Track daily self-talk, practice reframes, and design powerful questions.

"The words we choose become the worlds we inhabit."

As coaches, we are gardeners of language. We cultivate, nurture, prune, and seed transformation through words.

### Language I Carry: A Reflective Space for Coaches

- What three words do I speak to myself when I feel behind, unsure, or under pressure?
- What phrases from my upbringing shaped how I view success or failure?
- What metaphors do I repeat unconsciously—with clients, teams, or myself?
- What is a phrase I long to hear but rarely say to myself?
- If my language was a garden, what needs watering? What needs weeding?

### Coaching Language: From Default to Intentional

Default Language → Reframed Alternative

| Default Language | Reframed Alternative |
|---|---|
| "Why do you keep doing this?" | "What's the pattern you're noticing here?" |
| "You have to own this." | "Where might your power lie in this?" |
| "That's not how it works." | "How does this usually unfold for you?" |
| "You're overreacting." | "What feels tender here for you right now?" |
| "Calm down." | "Would you like to pause and breathe together?" |
| "You're too emotional." | "What is your emotion asking you to honor?" |

## Words That Calm, Ground, and Open

Words That Calm:

- "Let's take a breath before we go on."
- "You're not alone in this."
- "You don't need to figure it all out now. We're here together."
- "There's no rush. Let's give this some space."
- "I hear that this matters. Let's honor that first."

Words That Open:

- "What's something you haven't said aloud yet?"
- "If your body could speak, what would it say?"
- "What wants to be understood here & not solved?"
- "If we paused the story, what would you still feel?"

Words That Ground:

- "What do you need most right now: to talk, to sit, or to breathe?"
- "What truth are you holding that feels heavy?"
- "Can we give this moment the dignity it deserves?"

Words shape more than conversations; they shape inner landscapes. In coaching, a single phrase can soothe a storm or stir something long buried. As we explored, language doesn't just land in the mind; it resonates in the nervous system. The tone, timing, and texture of our words can either create safety or trigger survival.

But what happens after the words land? What do clients do with the emotional waves that rise in response?

That's where our journey now turns: into the world of emotions as even the most powerful insight can be swept away if the emotional current beneath it isn't understood.

Let's step into the deeper waters of emotional mastery.

# Chapter 3: Emotional Mastery: Surfing the Inner Waves

*Reclaiming agency, building resilience, and anchoring presence in the storms of high-performance.*

***"Feelings are much like waves. We can't stop them from coming, but we can choose which ones to surf."*** - *Jonatan Mårtensson*

**Words awaken.**
They stir memory, meaning, and emotion.
But once the words are spoken—what rises next often lives beyond them.
A shift in breath. A tightening in the chest.
This is where insight meets emotion—and where the real transformation begins.
Let's journey now into the heart of emotional mastery.

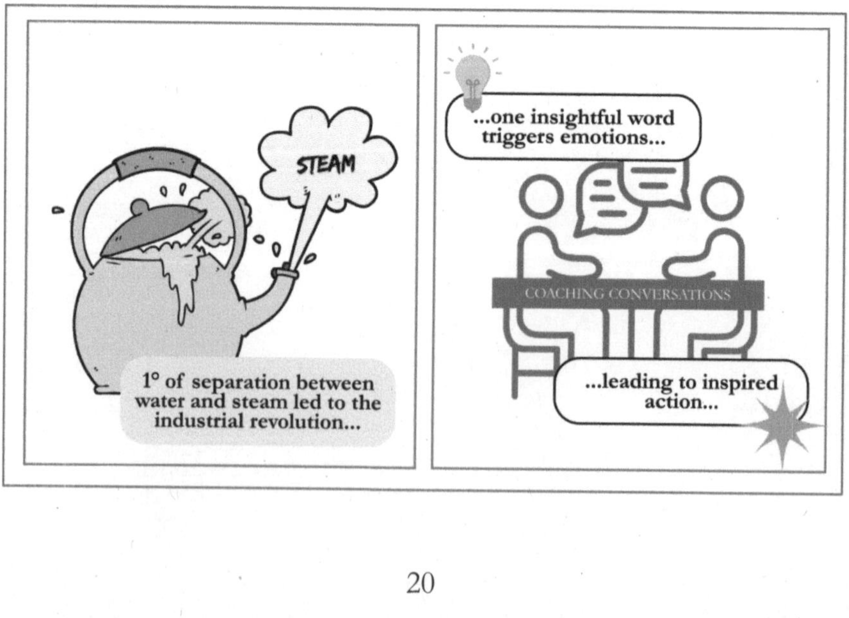

## Why Emotional Mastery Matters

In the heart of every conversation, beneath the plans, the performance, the perfectly rehearsed answers there is always emotion. Often unspoken, but always present.

Emotions are not interruptions to logic or professionalism. They are data, direction, and depth. They whisper what we care about, signal when something feels off, and shape how we experience the world. Yet, in many high-performance spaces; especially in leadership, emotions are either downplayed or misunderstood.

We call people "emotional" as if it's a flaw. We label sadness as weakness, anger as danger, and numbness as discipline. But the truth is that emotions are the language of aliveness. Without emotional awareness, even the most brilliant strategies can ring hollow. Without emotional congruence, connection becomes performance. And without emotional regulation, our power turns brittle.

This is why emotional mastery isn't just a coaching tool. It's a life skill. It's the foundation beneath presence, the bridge between knowing and becoming, and the anchor in moments of intensity, ambiguity, or fear.

Emotional Mastery does not mean suppression.
It means choice.
It means not being at the mercy of every inner wave, but learning to surf with awareness.
It means noticing the wave before it crashes and responding from center rather than from storm.

In coaching, emotional mastery allows us to attune to our clients without absorbing their intensity. In leadership, it enables us to communicate with clarity without collapsing into reactivity. And in personal growth, it helps us move from avoidance to alignment.

Every shift we seek on the outside; whether in behavior, decision-making, or relationships, is powered by a current within. If we cannot navigate that current, we stay in a loop of short-term change.

Before we explore how emotions can hijack our best intentions, let us pause to recognize this: emotional mastery is not an accessory to performance. It is the engine.

*When was the last time you responded from the center rather than the storm? And what shifted because of it?*

Let's pause and clear a common fog.

When people hear the phrase *"emotional mastery,"* they often imagine something it is not. A flawless calm. A surgical precision over feeling. A leader who never flinches, never falters, never lets a single emotion ripple the surface.

That is not mastery. That is performance.

Emotional mastery is not control.
Not the tight grip that keeps feelings caged behind the ribs.
Not the practiced smile that hides the storm beneath.
Control, when driven by fear, is not power; it is disconnection dressed as discipline.

It is not perfection, either.

Mastery doesn't mean we stop getting triggered. It doesn't mean we never cry in the boardroom, never feel jealousy or fear or grief. It doesn't mean we become immune to feeling.

Emotional mastery doesn't sterilize your humanness.
It simply deepens your relationship with it.

And it certainly is not disconnection.

Some people pride themselves on being "unemotional"; often, that just means they've learned to bypass. They move fast, stay sharp, keep things surface. Not because they don't feel; but because they're afraid of what they'll find if they slow down.

Avoidance wears many masks: professionalism, logic, ambition. But under the mask is a human asking to be heard.

The goal of emotional mastery isn't to build walls.
It's to create *inner spaciousness.*
The kind that lets you stay in the room with your whole self, without being consumed by it.

Mastery is the quiet knowing that says:

"I can feel this… and still choose how I move."

It's not about building a dam.
It's about learning to surf.
To ride the wave without being thrown by it.
To know when to lean in, when to steady yourself, and when to let go.

In coaching, this matters more than we often name.

Clients bring their waves into our space; sometimes crashing, sometimes frozen, sometimes so familiar they no longer recognize them as waves. If we equate emotional mastery with emotional neutrality, we miss the deeper invitation: to be a mirror, not a mask.

You don't have to be a blank slate.
You have to be still on shore.

Steady. Attuned. Safe enough for the client to meet themselves.

That's when the real work begins; not in tools, but in presence.
Not in control, but in clarity.
Not in fixing the feeling, but in listening to what it longs to reveal.

So, before we ask clients to stay with themselves,
we must ask: *Can I stay with me?*

## The Precision of Feeling: Emotional Granularity in Coaching

Most clients don't arrive at a coaching session with emotional clarity. They use general words: 'stressed', 'upset', 'angry': without fully grasping what lies beneath. Naming an emotion precisely changes how the brain processes it. This is the practice of *emotional granularity*; the ability to distinguish between nuanced emotional states with accuracy and depth.

Neuroscientist Lisa Feldman Barrett's research shows that people with high emotional granularity are more resilient, have better emotional regulation, and are less reactive under pressure. They're not overwhelmed by a blur of feeling; they can recognize whether what they're experiencing is frustration, disappointment, envy, or fatigue. And in that recognition, the emotional charge begins to soften.

As coaches, we can support this by gently guiding clients toward specificity. '*If that feeling had a texture or a color, what would it be?*' or '*Is it sadness, or is it something more like emptiness or grief?* 'Questions like these help clients step out of cognitive overdrive and into emotional precision.

### Tool for Coaches: The Emotion Wheel

Consider introducing clients to a visual tool like Plutchik's Wheel of Emotions or the Atlas of Emotions (by Paul Ekman); as a reflective aid.

You might say: '*Sometimes it helps to have language for what you're feeling. If you look at this wheel, do any of these words feel closer to what you're experiencing?*'

Naming emotions is not a minor act; it rewires the brain. When a client moves from "I'm overwhelmed" to "I'm torn between obligation and guilt," they gain traction. From there, choice becomes possible.

Emotional granularity deepens awareness. It also honors the complexity of being human; something no coaching model can capture, but presence can hold.

## When Emotions Hijack Our Best Intentions

Let me start by asking you something simple, yet powerful : have you ever felt completely thrown off by something as small as a tone of voice or a sudden email notification? One minute you're feeling productive and focused, the next, you're in full-blown reaction mode: tense, distracted, maybe even angry or anxious.

This is what we call emotional hijacking; and it's more common than we admit, especially for high-achievers who are always "on." A single email, an offhand comment, or an unexpected change can trigger an emotional response that feels out of our control. You might not even recognize it at first, but your body and mind have already shifted into overdrive, and suddenly, you're no longer in a place of choice; you're in reaction mode.

Maya Angelou once said, "You may not control all the events that happen to you, but you can decide not to be reduced by them."

That's the heart of emotional mastery; responding from awareness rather than reacting from habit.

## What Emotions Are Really Telling Us

When we think of emotional mastery, we often begin with the visible: outbursts, shutdowns, hijacks. And while those moments matter, emotions carry far more than reaction. They carry meaning.

Every emotion is a messenger.
It may arrive as tightness in the chest or heat in the jaw.

But underneath the physiological signal is something quieter and deeper:
a belief, a memory, a value, a fear, a longing.

Emotions rise not only when we're threatened; but when something we care about is touched.

Anger might signal that a value has been violated.
Sadness might speak of something precious that's been lost.
Anxiety might be guarding an identity we fear will be judged.
Even numbness has a message: This is too much right now.

This is why emotional mastery isn't about suppression.
It's about listening.

Emotions drive people. People drive performance. (Six Seconds)

And behind every "What do you want to do?" lies the invisible "Why do you want to do what you want to do?" Or "What drives this need?"

As coaches, when we stay curious about the emotion; not just the story, we help clients reconnect with their deepest drivers. We begin to notice that what may sound like procrastination may be fear of rejection. What looks like ambition may be a need to be seen. What feels like resistance may actually be self-protection.

Emotions aren't barriers to overcome.
They are the truth trying to reach the surface.

And when we learn to ride the wave of the emotion instead of resisting it, we uncover the wisdom beneath it.

## Empathy and the Power of Mirror Neurons

Empathy is often described as the cornerstone of human connection—an ability to step into another's world, feel what they feel, and witness them without judgment. In coaching, empathy is not simply a method; it is the very presence that opens doors within the client. Yet, beneath this invisible exchange lies a fascinating biological truth. The ability to attune to another's experience is not just emotional—it is neurobiological.

At the core of this process are mirror neurons—a network of specialized brain cells discovered in the 1990s by neuroscientists studying monkeys. These neurons activate both when we perform an action and when we observe someone else performing the same action. But their function goes far beyond mimicry. In humans, mirror neurons play a significant role in emotional resonance. They allow us to sense, almost instinctively, what another person is feeling.

When a coach is deeply present—regulated, grounded, and attuned—the client's nervous system begins to mirror that state. This phenomenon, often referred to as limbic resonance, creates a sense of psychological safety in the coaching space. The client may not understand why they feel more open or emotionally accessible in our presence, but their system recognizes the calm, coherent state we offer. In that stillness, defenses begin to melt.

*"I felt like you understood me without me having to explain everything."* — A phrase we hear often as coaches. It is the language of resonance.

This resonance does not arise from doing more. It emerges from being more present. When we slow down and allow ourselves to truly witness the client—beyond their words, into the subtle inflections, body language, and energy—we are engaging our mirror neurons in service of their transformation. We are meeting them not only with intellect, but with biology, heart, and deep listening.

Interestingly, mirror neurons also respond to intention. When our presence carries compassion, curiosity, and respect, our client's mirror system reflects back that emotional tone. It's a silent conversation between nervous systems. And it is in this unspoken space that breakthroughs often emerge—not through analysis, but through felt safety.

This understanding adds a new layer to coaching presence. We are not only listening with our minds but with our entire neurosensory being. Our breath, posture, eye contact, and internal emotional state all communicate safety or threat. This is where the real alchemy of coaching lives—not in our tools, but in our presence.

*Practice: Resonance Check-In*

After your next conversation, take five quiet minutes to reflect:

- Did I feel emotionally aligned with my client at any point?
- Was I aware of my own inner state throughout the session?
- When did the client seem to shift—relax, open up, or access a deeper insight?
- Could that have been a moment of mirror resonance?

Cultivating empathy through mirror neurons is not about effort. It is about awareness. As we refine our presence, we naturally become more resonant. Our biology, quite literally, supports transformation.

## The Coach as Anchor: Presence in Emotional Waters

Coaches often ask: *How do I help my client stay present, make conscious choices, and lead from the inside out?* The answer starts with us.

Coaches are the anchor in the emotional tide. While clients bring stories, goals, and uncertainty, what they often crave is a space where they can feel fully met. A space where they don't have to perform clarity, or hide confusion. Where they can simply be human.

And for that to happen, coaches must learn to hold emotional intensity without being swept away by it.

Emotional mastery begins with us.
Not in technique, but in nervous system integrity.

It's easy to be present when things feel easy. But when a client's voice cracks, when anger enters the room, when silence stretches into discomfort; that's when our inner steadiness matters most.

The coach is not just a guide; they are the emotional container. And to hold space for another's complexity, they must first be able to hold our own. Emotional mastery begins not with technique, but with presence. And presence is born of emotional intelligence.

That's what we bring into every session.
The quiet clarity to notice when our own edges are being pressed.
The strength to sit with discomfort without softening the truth or rushing to fix.
The humility to listen not just to words, but to what rises between them.

Presence is more than being there. It's 'how' we are there. It's the moment we soften our breath instead of rushing to solve. The moment we stay curious when judgment threatens to rise. This isn't a conscious performance. It's attunement and alignment.

Daniel Goleman's work on emotional intelligence speaks to this: the capacity to notice, regulate, empathize, and connect; first within us, and then with others. As coaches, we bring all of that into the room as an embodied practice.

We don't co-regulate by staying neutral. We co-regulate by staying grounded. We model what we hope our clients will practice: being with emotion, instead of reacting to it. We regulate to appear composed, so that our stillness becomes an anchor.
We attune because we're trained to, and because we care to.

And at the heart of it all, we return; again, to a simple inner rhythm that helps us stay in integrity while holding space for others.

Know yourself. Choose yourself. Give yourself.
Not as a method. As a way of walking in.

When a coach lives from this place, the session becomes more than a conversation.
It becomes a moment of truth, trust, and transformation.

*Listening as Emotional Presence*

Coaching is not a transaction of thoughts.
It's a conversation between *whole people.* We're not just listening for words.
We're listening for what's alive.

The subtle change in tone. The held breath.
The shift in pace when a truth edges closer to the surface.

These are not distractions; they're invitations.

We're not interpreting. We're integrating.
We don't explain emotion, we acknowledge it.
To reflect energy, not to analyze it.
To witness, not to fix.

And so, emotional mastery is not just something we guide our clients toward; it's something we practice in real time.

When the coach becomes the anchor, the session becomes the shore.
A place the client can return to.
And more importantly, a place where they learn to return to *themselves.*

## The 4 A's of Emotional Mastery – A Cycle of Emotional Leadership

*Before we dive in, think of the 4 A's as a compass; to navigate emotion with presence and leadership.*

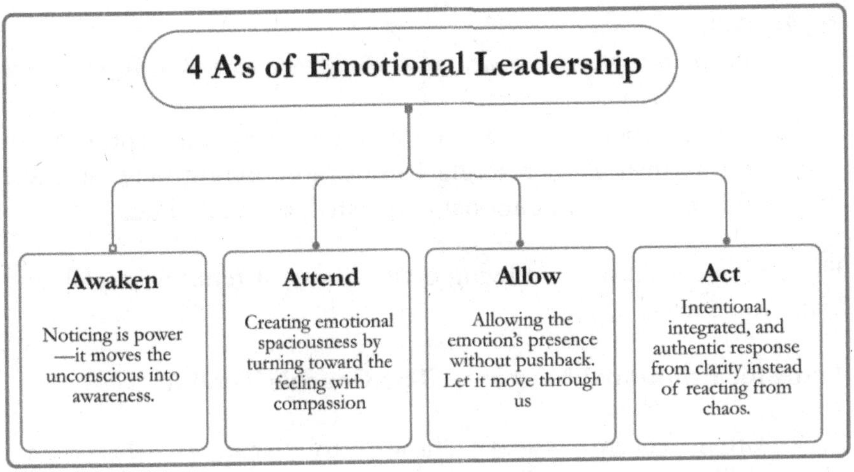


Think of this as a compass for navigating emotional intensity; to move through it and not to eliminate it,

1. **Awaken**
   *What am I feeling right now? Where is it in my body? What triggered it?*
   Most emotional hijacks begin below the radar. This step is about slowing down the moment enough to notice what's true. Noticing is power: it moves the unconscious into awareness.

2. **Attend**
   *Can I stay with this emotion without rushing to fix it? What is this feeling trying to tell me?*
   This is the step of creating emotional spaciousness. We turn toward the feeling with compassion. We let it speak without interrupting. We let it be without making it a problem.

3. **Allow**
   *Can I accept this feeling as part of my experience, without shame or resistance?*
   Allowing is presence without pushback. We don't try to reframe too quickly. We let the emotion move through us, trusting it has a rhythm. Allowing is how we soften into what is.

4. **Act**
   *From this grounded place, what choice feels aligned with who I am becoming?*
   This is where the power returns; the client can respond from clarity instead of reacting from chaos. Action here isn't just functional; it's intentional, integrated, and authentic.

This isn't a checklist. It's a living cycle. A way of returning; again and again, to yourself.

**Tools for Emotional Mastery – The Coach's Toolkit**

I've often been asked 'how' to achieve this state There are practices that I built into my routine that are small, sacred invitations to return to self. To choose awareness over reaction. Stillness over speed. Compassion over control.

**Neuroscience Anchors**

- Micro-pauses engage the prefrontal cortex and interrupt reaction.
- Naming emotions reduces amygdala activation—*'Name it to tame it."*
- Repetition builds resilience—rituals create neural grooves of safety.

**Somatic Tools**

- Feet on the ground: "Can you feel the support beneath you?"
- Orienting: Turn the head slowly. Remind the brain: *you are safe.*
- Breath ratios: Inhale 4, exhale 6. A biological return to calm.
- Hand on heart: A silent reminder that the body knows how to soften.

**Coach as Mirror**

- Slow your pace. Breathe.
- Name the moment: *"You paused there. What showed up?"*

- Stay steady in the storm. Co-regulate. Be the tuning fork.

**Client Practices Between Sessions**

- The 4 A's journal: A daily page to unpack difficult moments.
- Anchor word: One guiding word per week: "Centered." "Spacious."
- Micro rituals: A breath before speaking. A pause before replying.
- Somatic check-ins: "What is your body saying about this?"

**Common Resistance**

- Avoidance: Talking around the emotion. Invite sensation.
- Over-identification: "I am this feeling." Offer space to witness it.
- Shame or collapse: Hold softly. Normalize the messiness of being human.
- Frustration at relapse: "You noticed. That *is* the shift."

## Practicing Emotional Leadership: Case Studies from the Coaching Room

**From Burnout to Boundaries**

Name: Gemma

Profile: High Performing Product Lead in a Startup

Gemma didn't come to coaching to grow.
She came because she was on the edge of collapse. She was the one who always delivered. Nights blurred into launch cycles. Her calendar had no white space. Her inbox showed no mercy. And somewhere in between the strategy calls and school pick-ups, she had stopped feeling anything except tired.

In our first session, she smiled tightly and said,
*"I just need to be more efficient with my time."*

But as we slowed down, her voice betrayed her.
There was an ache she was trying to hide beneath that productivity.
A sadness she hadn't named.

She was constantly moving, so she wouldn't feel how lost she'd become.

We began small.

I didn't ask her to change her schedule.
I asked her to notice her breath.
We practiced the micro-pause: one intentional breath before opening her laptop.
She began placing a hand on her belly during meetings to ground herself.

I asked her to journal at night : not about tasks, but about emotions:

- *"What did I feel today?"*
- *"Where did I abandon myself?"*
- *"What moment gave me breath?"*

It wasn't easy. She was used to performing. Even in reflection.

Sometimes, she came to sessions and said,
*"I don't know what I'm feeling. I just feel blank."*
So we stayed there. In the blankness.
Because even numbness has wisdom.

Slowly, the numbness gave way to tears.
Tears that had been waiting for a safe place to fall.

She began to realize that her exhaustion wasn't just from work; it was from pretending not to need anything.

Her turning point came not with a breakdown, but a decision.

After a particularly intense sprint, she told her team,
*"I'm taking Friday off. No meetings. No apologies. I'll be offline."*

It was the first time she had drawn a boundary without guilt.

That weekend, she didn't go anywhere.
She sat on her balcony with a book. She watched the sky change color.
She let silence come in like a tide.

And something in her body whispered: *I'm still here.*

Over the next few months, she practiced the 4 A's without naming them:

- Awaken: Recognizing the tightness in her shoulders before meetings.
- Attend: Sitting with her overwhelm instead of pushing through.
- Allow: Letting herself cry after difficult conversations.
- Act: Choosing not to answer late-night messages; and instead, choosing herself.

Her team noticed something different.

She was still competent. Still clear.
But now she was available.
To tasks and to connection.

One of her peers said,
*"You used to feel intense. Now you feel intentional."*

Six months later, Gemma said to me,
*"I didn't change my job. I changed my relationship with myself."*
*"I still get tired; but now I know how to return."*

She didn't burn out. She burned away the version of herself who believed being needed was the same as being worthy.

She became more than productive. She became present.

*Reflection: What is your body asking for that your mind has been overriding?*

**Emotional Presence at the Top: "I Don't Do Vulnerability"**

Name: Raghav

Profile: Senior VP of a Global Tech Company

Raghav was the kind of leader people followed with their heads, but not always with their hearts. He was known for precision, intellect, and relentless delivery. His team met deadlines. His meetings ran like clockwork. His presentations left little room for challenge. All of the perfection didn't leave much room for him.

He didn't come to coaching not because of a crisis; he came because his CEO had suggested he *"work on emotional intelligence."* That phrase alone made him bristle.

*"I don't do vulnerability,"* he said flatly in our first session. *"That's not my lane."*

So, we didn't start with vulnerability.
We started with noticing…

Noticing how his chest tightened every time someone gave feedback.
Noticing the exhaustion behind his sharp efficiency.
Noticing how much energy went into controlling his image.

He was skilled at navigating complexity; but unfamiliar with navigating his own emotional terrain.

One afternoon, we paused mid-session as he shared a team conflict. I asked,
*"What are you feeling in this moment- not about them, but about being here, in this conversation?"*

He was silent. His breath was shallow.

Then, slowly:
*"Uncomfortable. But… relieved. Like I don't have to perform right now."*

That was the crack.

We worked with the 4 A's. We explored how leadership isn't about always knowing.
We practiced presence before precision. Listening before responding.
He began showing up differently in meetings; not softer, but more available.

A month later, a senior team member told him,
*"You feel more real these days. Like we're finally working with you, not just your title."*

He didn't lose his edge. He gained his depth.

He still led decisively, now with emotional range.
With courage to say, *"I don't know,"* or *"That didn't land well,"* or *"Let's pause before we push this further."*

He became a leader people trusted for presence; not just for outcomes

*Reflection: What might shift in your leadership if you brought more emotional awareness into the room?*

**Relearning Joy: "I Forgot I Could Feel This"**

Name: Aanya

Profile: Management Consultant

Aanya was a brilliant consultant, widely respected in her field for her clarity, logic, and tactical brilliance. She was organized, sharp, and self-sufficient.
And in her words, *"very good at staying above the emotional clutter."*

She didn't come to coaching for healing.
She came because she had everything; and couldn't feel anything.

No crisis. No chaos. Just a sense of quiet disconnection.

"I laugh with my team, but I don't feel joy.
I spend time with my family, but it feels... rehearsed.
I know how to function. But I don't know if I'm really living."

We explored the pain along with the pause.
The numbness.
The subtle ache of having muted too much for too long.

In one session, I invited her to recall a moment in life she had felt deeply alive.
She hesitated. Then shared a memory of singing as a teenager; alone, in her room, full voice, no audience.

Her eyes welled up. *"I forgot I could feel this."*

So, we began there.
Not fixing, not forcing - But noticing the small stirrings of emotion when joy, play, or longing came into the room.

I asked her to create a "joy file." Not a gratitude list. Not goals. Just moments that felt alive.
A child laughing in a café.
Rain on her window.
The color yellow.

Each week, she added one moment.
And each week, the numbness loosened its grip.

She said one day, *"I used to think I was strong because I didn't need anything. Now I realize I'm stronger because I can feel everything, and not lose myself."*

She didn't leave her job. She didn't change her world.
She returned to it; with color.

Reflection: *Have you mistaken emotional detachment for strength? What part of you is waiting to feel again?*

Let me leave you with these thoughts……

**The Shore We Return To**

There is a rhythm beneath all the noise.
Beneath the deadlines and decisions,
beneath the roles we play and the masks we hold in place—
there is breath.
There is stillness.
There is the quiet knowing that we are not here to conquer our emotions,
but to listen to them.

Not every wave is a warning.
Some are invitations.
To soften. To pause. To feel.

We do not need to brace against every tide.
We can learn to ride it.
To let it rise, and fall, and rise again
without losing ourselves in the swell.

Because emotional mastery is not about getting it right.
It's about coming home. Again and again.
To the truth that we are not fragile.
We are fluid. We are fierce. We are whole.

We are the shore we've been searching for.

## A Note on Coaching vs. Therapy.

It's important to pause here and name something clearly:

This work is not therapy.
It is coaching.

While therapy often explores the past to diagnose, process, and heal, coaching listens to the past with compassion; only to bring the client more fully into the present, so that they can move forward with clarity and intention.

We don't analyze emotion. We acknowledge it.
We don't treat dysfunction. We cultivate awareness.
We don't stay in the story. We partner in the shift.

A coach holds space not to fix what was,
but to amplify who the client is becoming.

That means emotion may enter the room, but we meet it as wisdom trying to surface & not as a wound. That's the heart of emotional mastery: responding from awareness rather than reacting from habit.

# Part Two

# Coaching The Intangible: The EQ Advantage

In the chapters so far, we've explored how emotions shape behavior, drive performance, and influence the choices leaders make under pressure. We've seen how emotional mastery isn't about suppressing feelings; it's about honoring them, understanding them, and skillfully navigating through them. We examined the difference between reacting and responding, and how a coach's role is not to offer direction, but to hold space for inner clarity to emerge.

But there's another layer. A softer, subtler dimension that lives beneath the surface of performance—the realm of what cannot always be named, but is always felt. This is the space where real transformation begins.

Not with tools, but with presence.
Not with strategies, but with sensing.

Welcome to the deeper dimension of coaching, Coaching the Intangible; where emotional intelligence becomes more than a concept. It becomes a way of perceiving, relating, and being. This section explores the quiet power of EQ as the anchor for profound, soul-level shifts in clients.

# Chapter 4: The Key to Deep Shifts

***"It takes something more than intelligence to act intelligently."***
*- Fyodor Dostoyevsky*

We begin with the foundation: The Key to Deep Shifts. The most powerful tool in a coach's arsenal is emotional intelligence.

Emotional intelligence creates the conditions for insight, integration, and inner evolution. If emotional intelligence is the current beneath visible waters, coaching is the art of swimming in it; with grace, presence, and trust. As we move deeper into the realm of the intangible, we now ask: what truly enables lasting inner change?

The answer lies in the quiet, luminous force of emotional intelligence.

At its heart, EQ is not a set of techniques—it's a way of being. It invites us to turn inward, to listen between the lines of our thoughts, to feel the textures of our emotional landscape. It's like holding up a lantern in the fog; we may not see the full path, but we start to notice what's right in front of us—and that awareness changes everything.

Let's explore the five core elements of EQ:

1. Self-awareness
2. Self-regulation
3. Motivation
4. Empathy
5. Social skills

We'll look at these as inner muscles we strengthen through coaching. These aren't just traits of effective leaders; they are portals to the self. Each one opens a different doorway:

Self-awareness whispers: Pause. Look within. Know thyself.
Self-regulation teaches: You are not your reaction.
Motivation calls: Lead with purpose, not pressure.
Empathy leans in: Feel with, not just for.
Social skills remind us: Connection is the true currency.

These capacities often feel intangible, just like subtle shifts in energy, a change in tone, a pause before a response. But as neuroscience confirms, they are also deeply embodied. New neural pathways are formed. Habits are rewired. Leadership evolves not from the outside in, but from the inside out.

As coaches, we hold space for these shifts. We ask questions that stir reflection, we mirror the unseen, and we stay with the silence long enough for something new to emerge. In the chapters ahead, we'll unpack techniques to strengthen these dimensions of EQ in clients and witness what happens when they begin to lead, live, and love from that place.

Deep shifts don't announce themselves with fireworks. They arrive like a change in the wind; felt more than seen. And EQ is how we learn to listen.

Before we explore these qualities in depth, let's pause and consider how emotional intelligence lives in ideas, in experiences, how it shows up in the everyday moments that define how we lead, relate, and respond.

## The EQ Lotus

To bring this into focus, I offer a model I call The EQ Lotus™. It distills the essence of emotional intelligence into five foundational capacities each one a petal that unfolds from the dense layers of self-protection into clarity, resilience, and connection.

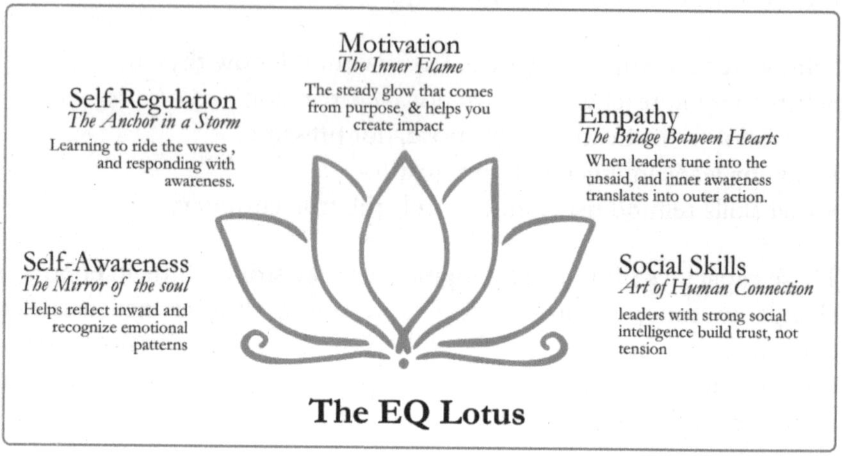


At the heart of every deep shift lie five core elements, the petals of the EQ Lotus™

This model is designed to be a visual and emotional map for both clients and coaches. Like the lotus, each petal grows from the muddy waters of our conditioning, offering clarity, peace, and purpose as we deepen our self-awareness.

**Self-Awareness: The Mirror of the Soul**

Imagine standing beside a still lake and seeing your reflection with total honesty. Self-awareness is like that—a clear look without judgment. A client once said, "I never realized how much my fear of judgment was shaping my decisions." That moment—raw, vulnerable, and real—became the beginning of her transformation.

- The Neuroscientific Lens: Self-awareness activates the brain's default mode network, helping us reflect inward and recognize emotional patterns.
- Reflection: *When was the last time you saw yourself clearly, without filters or fear?*

Before we can shape how we show up in the world, we must first understand what drives us from within. And that brings us to the next petal: our emotional anchor.

**Self-Regulation: The Anchor in a Storm**

Emotions are waves. Self-regulation is learning to ride them, not drown in them. It's not about suppressing anger or fear but about responding with awareness. One client once shared, "*Earlier, I reacted. Now, I respond.*"

That shift, from impulse to intention, is the real magic.

- The Neuroscientific Lens: Regulation engages the prefrontal cortex, allowing us to override amygdala-driven reactivity and make conscious choices.
- Reflection:
  *What emotion tends to hijack your calm—and how do you usually meet it?*

With self-awareness and regulation in place, we begin to clear the emotional clutter. What emerges next is the quiet fire, our deeper drive.

**Motivation: The Inner Flame**

This isn't the spark that burns out quickly. It's the steady glow that comes from purpose. When clients connect to this inner flame, they stop chasing promotions and start creating impact. Their energy becomes focused, meaningful, and magnetic.

- The Neuroscientific Lens: Dopamine pathways tied to intrinsic motivation fire when actions align with personal meaning, fueling sustained effort.
- Reflection:
  *What drives you beneath the surface? Is it aligned with who you're becoming?*

Purpose without connection can become performance. The next petal asks us to reach beyond ourselves; to truly feel with others.

**Empathy: The Bridge Between Hearts**

Empathy is not just "walking in someone's shoes." It's feeling the gravel beneath their feet. When leaders learn to tune into what's not being said, workplaces become human again. Meetings shift from performance reviews to honest conversations. Teams breathe easier.

- The Neuroscientific Lens: Mirror neurons in the brain help us sense and simulate the emotions of others—forming the basis of empathy.
- Reflection*:*
  *When did you last truly hear someone, beyond their words?*

Empathy, when embodied, naturally paves the way for the final petal, where we translate all this inner awareness into outer action.

**Social Skills: The Art of Human Connection**

Think of a conductor guiding an orchestra. Each cue, each pause, each gesture—creating harmony. Social skills work the same way. Whether resolving conflict, inspiring action, or giving feedback, leaders with strong social intelligence build trust, not tension.

- The Neuroscientific Lens: Oxytocin, the bonding hormone, increases when we engage in trust-building behaviors, enhancing team dynamics and communication.
- Reflection:
  *Where in your life could you lead with more connection than correction?*

Understanding the five petals of the EQ Lotus™ gives us a map. But coaching emotional intelligence isn't just about recognizing these elements—it's about nurturing them in real time, in real people.

So how do we, as coaches, become cultivators of this inner garden?

What follows are practices and frameworks that support the unfolding of these petals—tools to help clients feel, reflect, realign, and grow.

## Coaching to Cultivate EQ: Tilling the Inner Soil

As coaches, we are gardeners of the unseen. We don't fix, we nurture. While each client's journey is unique, the REVEAL model offers a gentle structure to guide emotional breakthroughs.

### The REVEAL Coaching Framework

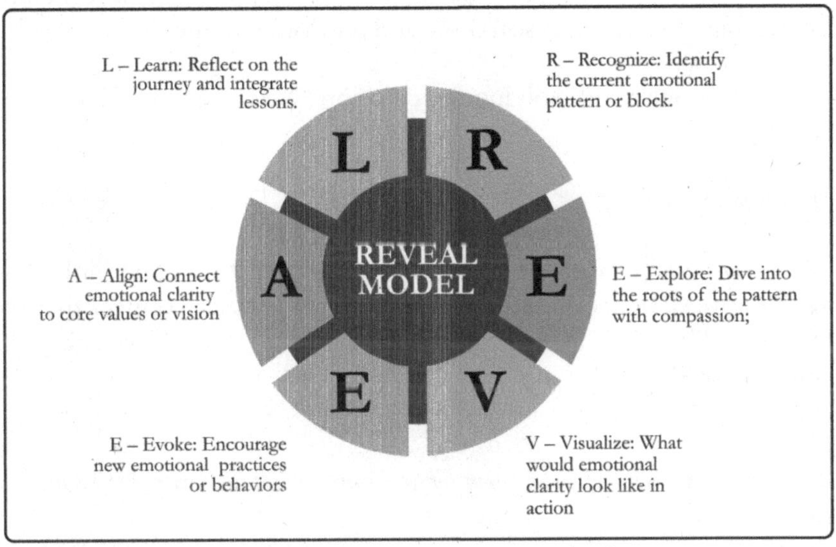


For instance, one client visualized what confidence would *feel* like in her body before a presentation—steady breath, relaxed posture, warm voice. That image became a touchstone for her new way of showing up.

## Tools & Exercises to Grow EQ in Clients

### Awareness Journals:

Encourage clients to track emotional patterns. Over time, these patterns become like constellations—they guide, they speak, they reveal.

Every emotion is a messenger. Anger might signal a boundary crossed. Sadness may reveal a need for connection. Anxiety can point to a desire for control or clarity. When we help clients explore the need behind the feeling, the emotion softens—and wisdom emerges.

As coaches, we're not solving the emotion. We're decoding its language.

*"If this feeling could speak, what would it ask for?"*

*The Neuroscientific Lens:* The insula, a part of the brain linked to interoception, helps us perceive emotional shifts and connect them to meaning. The more we engage in this, the more fluently we speak the language of the body.

*Reflection:*
*What emotion shows up most often for you—and what need might it be pointing to?*

### Role Reversal Exercises

Especially useful for building empathy. One leader wrote an apology letter from their team's perspective. That single act softened years of rigidity.

Emotional patterns are like grooves in a record—automatic, familiar, and often outdated. One way to support clients in rewriting these grooves is through micro-rituals: a small, symbolic act that signals a new way of being.

A clenched fist becomes an open palm. A held breath becomes a sigh of release. A critical thought gets paused with a whisper, *"That's the old story."*

It's not about forcing change. It's about interrupting autopilot with intention.

Coaching Tip:
Invite the client to create a symbolic gesture or phrase they can use in the moment a reactive pattern arises, something simple, meaningful, and grounding.

*Reflection:*
*What habitual emotional response are you ready to interrupt—and what new response could you begin to rehearse instead?*

**Pause Practices**

Simple breathwork or mindfulness rituals before high-stakes moments. Even a 30-second pause can shift a conversation from collision to connection.

The pause is sacred ground. In that brief space, we move from unconscious reaction to intentional presence. A pause doesn't have to be long, it just has to be deliberate. A hand over the heart. A breath into the belly. A silent reminder: *"Choose clarity, not control."*

A senior leader once told me, "*I thought pausing would slow me down. Turns out, it was the only thing that made me effective.*"

*Reflection:*
*"What does it feel like to pause before your next word?"*

## Inner Dialogue Scripts

### Giving Voice to the Silent Selves

Sometimes, the clearest insights come when we give form to our internal parts. Invite the client to write short letters or dialogues between their emotional "selves"—the one who feels fear, the one who holds courage, the one who hides, the one who dreams.

This practice invites self-empathy, clarity, and integration.

You might ask:

*"If your fear and your courage had a conversation, what would they say to each other?"*

These voices aren't in conflict—they are trying to harmonize.

*Reflection:*
*What part of you have you been silencing—and what does it want to say?*

### Value Alignment Tools

Help clients rediscover what truly matters. When they find their "why," the "how" becomes more graceful.

When clients are disconnected from their values, they drift. But when they anchor in what matters most—truth, impact, connection, creativity—they gain direction. Not externally imposed direction, but inner alignment.

Help them map key values and track how aligned their current roles or relationships are. When leaders know their "why," the "how" becomes clearer and more effortless.

One client realized her burnout stemmed not from overwork, but from working out of alignment with her core value: creativity.

*Reflection:*
*"When did you last feel fully alive? What value was present in that moment?"*

**Somatic Check-Ins**

Invite clients to tune into their body's signals—a clenched jaw, tight shoulders, fluttering chest. The body always knows before the mind catches up.

The body tells the truth before the mind catches up. A clenched jaw can reveal unspoken frustration. A tight chest may hold unacknowledged fear. A flutter in the gut might be excitement—or dread.

Invite clients to scan their body and name what they feel. You might ask, "Where in your body is this emotion sitting?" This simple act brings clients back into presence—and often, into clarity.

*Reflection:*
*"What sensation is calling your attention right now?"*

Which of these practices speaks to you—and how might you bring it into your coaching or leadership?

**Case Study: The Empathy Gap**

Name: Michael

Profile: Tech leader

When Michael came to me for coaching, he was clearly a brilliant leader. Sharp-minded but emotionally distant. His team admired his competence but feared his presence. Feedback described him as "intimidating," "hard to reach," "unapproachable."

In our initial sessions, Michael dismissed empathy entirely. "*I pay people to perform, not to be understood,*" he said with finality. That wall of belief had been constructed long ago, brick by brick through childhood experiences where vulnerability was met with criticism, and achievement was the only accepted form of connection.

As our coaching unfolded, I noticed subtle openings: a softening of tone when speaking about his daughter, a hesitation when confronted with the emotional fatigue of his team. These became entry points. We leaned into the REVEAL model: exploring, evoking, aligning. One powerful breakthrough came during a role-reversal exercise. Michael wrote an internal memo from his team's perspective.

Reading it aloud, he paused midway.

"They're afraid of me," he whispered. "And I never meant to lead that way."

That moment of raw clarity cracked something open. We practiced active listening and emotional acknowledgment. I invited him to begin meetings with one question: "How are you feeling coming into this conversation?" Simple, but revolutionary for him.

Six months later, his team began using a new word to describe him: approachable. One team member shared, *"Michael listens now. He doesn't rush. We feel seen."*

Michael didn't just shift behaviors.
He rewired his internal narrative: from leadership as dominance to leadership as *presence.*

He didn't become someone else.
He became more himself.

## Emotional Intelligence: Imperative Skill for the Coach

Emotional intelligence in coaching is not just the ability to read cues or manage reactions. At its highest level, it is a compassionate witnessing of the client's full humanity, while staying fully anchored in our own. It is awareness without absorption, holding without collapse.

Masterful coaches bring emotional intelligence into the room not only as a skillset but as a *state of being.* It shows up in the way we breathe with the client's pace, track shifts in tone, and notice when their eyes reveal something their words avoid. It shows up in how we stay with the silence after a moment of truth, or how we soften when a client struggles to forgive themselves.

This is where emotional intelligence meets mindfulness. The emotionally intelligent coach is not reactive; they are responsive. Grounded in presence, they notice their own emotional stirrings but choose where and how to act. Mindfulness doesn't numb the emotional field—it illuminates it.

By cultivating emotional intelligence through mindful attention, we become skilled at navigating moments of emotional charge: those subtle thresholds where transformation waits. These moments often require nothing more than being deeply there, unflinching and available, as the client meets something they usually avoid.

## Emotional Regulation

Emotional regulation is less about self control and more about inner spaciousness. It is the capacity to remain still and clear, even when a client's story touches our own, or when an unexpected emotional wave arises in the session.

This is not emotional detachment; it is disciplined presence. The coach feels, but does not flinch. Listens, but does not rush to soothe. Coaches with high emotional regulation know how to metabolize their own feelings silently, so that they can continue to serve the client's unfolding process.

This inner steadiness becomes an anchor. It tells the client; wordlessly that they are safe to unravel, safe to not have it all together, safe to be fully seen. The emotionally regulated coach is a calm nervous system in the room. And that calmness transmits, beyond language; through tone, through pacing, through breath. It invites co-regulation, and over time, empowers the client to find that same emotional ground within themselves.

## The Emotional Risk of Deep Coaching

Coaching at depth is emotionally expensive. It invites the client into vulnerable terrain: grief, uncertainty, longing, shame, hope. But it also requires the coach to meet that terrain with a rare kind of strength: the strength to remain soft.

There is a risk in allowing emotional depth. The risk of being touched, of not knowing, of saying the thing that might change everything. And yet, this risk is sacred. When the coach allows emotional exposure, both their own and the client's; without needing to fix or hide, something alchemical happens. The space becomes real. Trust becomes cellular.

In these moments, coaching stops being a process and becomes a portal.

This is where emotional intelligence deepens into emotional wisdom. The coach doesn't analyze what the emotion means; they honor what it reveals. They allow it to shape the session in ways logic alone never could.

### Adaptability and Cultural Sensitivity in the Emotional Field

Emotionally intelligent coaching must be *adaptable.* No two emotional landscapes are the same. What feels expressive to one client may feel invasive to another. What seems avoidant in one culture may be considered dignified restraint in another.

Adaptability allows the coach to meet the client where they are: not just emotionally, but contextually. It's the flexibility to shift our pace, tone, and even silence to honor the client's emotional language. And it's the humility to recognize that our framework of expression may not be theirs.

Cultural competence, then, becomes an extension of emotional intelligence. It is not just awareness of diversity, but reverence for it. The emotionally intelligent coach is not only fluent in emotions; they are sensitive to how those emotions are held, revealed, or masked in different cultural and personal contexts.

Adaptability is the coach's ability to shift; not because the process demands it, but because the person in front of them does. It is the intuitive tuning that comes from paying close attention to the words, but to the space around them. Emotionally intelligent coaches adjust their rhythm, their tone, even their silence, based on the client's signals.

Adaptability and cultural sensitivity are not add-ons to emotional intelligence. They are expressions of it. When practiced with awareness and humility, they allow the coaching space to become not only emotionally safe, but personally relevant.

This is what makes emotional intelligence invisible. It's not what the coach says; it's what the client feels in their presence: safety, dignity, permission, trust.

## The Heart of It

EQ isn't about being nice.
It's about being awake.
It's not about control.
It's about clarity.

And it's not something we teach.
It's something we embody, and invite others into.

When we, as coaches, nurture emotional intelligence in our clients, we are not just shaping behavior; we are reshaping perception itself. We are shifting the very lens through which they see others, make decisions, and meet the world.

This is the heart of coaching the intangible.
It is what makes change last.
What makes it real.

The deepest shifts are rarely loud.
They arrive as stillness.
They arrive as a kind of presence.
They arrive when we listen with our whole being.

*That, dear reader, is the key to deep, lasting, soul-level shifts.*

# Chapter 5: Deep Presence & Silence: The #1 Coaching Skills

***"The truth is known in silence, be still and know."*** *- Leonard Jacobson*

## The Still-Point Beneath the Surface

Picture a lotus pond at dawn. The surface is glass-still. Clouds drift across like unhurried thoughts, dragonflies skim the water, yet nothing disturbs the deeper quiet below. That quiet is what I believe is deep presence: the still-point a coach cultivates so that another human being can hear their own wisdom ripple up from the depths.

For years we believed excellent coaching meant asking brilliant questions. Then neuroscience caught up with experience and whispered otherwise: *regulation is contagious.* A coach's nervous system, steady or scattered, entrains the client's own. When we settle into that pond-like stillness, mirror-neurons invite the client to do the same. Insight becomes possible not because we are clever, but because we are calm.

This is where presence begins: not with what we say, but with who we are when we say nothing.

## The Quiet Skill That Changes Everything

In the world of coaching, we talk a lot about tools, questions, models, frameworks. But the coaches who create lasting impact all seem to carry something else. It's harder to define. You feel it more than you see it.

It's presence and energy.

Presence is not just being in the room; it's being fully in the moment, without being consumed by it. That subtle but critical distinction is what allows us to be deeply involved with our clients, but never entangled in their storms. It's what allows us to care deeply, yet detach from needing a specific outcome.

*Presence is when a coach is involved but not entangled. It needs a certain level of detachment from the outcome.*

This is not detachment as indifference. It is spacious. It is the grounded confidence that the client's journey is theirs to walk, and ours to witness.

Presence allows us to trust the process, especially when nothing visible seems to be happening.

And that is when transformation often begins.

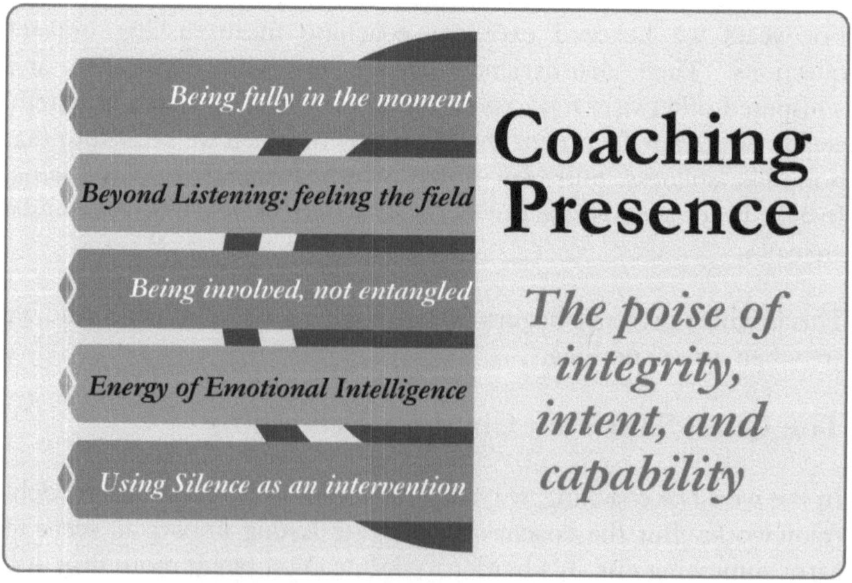

## Beyond Listening: Feeling the Field

Most people think listening is about the ears. In coaching, listening is done with the entire nervous system.

You listen with your breath.
You listen with your spine.
You listen with the space between words and the heaviness behind silences.

Deep presence turns listening into a full-body awareness. You notice the shift in tone, the slight hesitation, the emotional tremor beneath "*I'm fine.*" You pick up on contractions in their field; subtle signals that something isn't aligned, that a truth is trying to surface.

You don't chase these signals.
You wait.
You soften.
You trust.

That's what presence teaches: to trust the invisible.

## The Art of Being Involved but Not Entangled

One of the greatest marks of emotional maturity, both in coaching and in leadership—is the ability to be *fully with* someone without being pulled into their emotion or story.

*Involvement without entanglement* is a discipline. It's a muscle we strengthen over time. And it begins with noticing our own patterns:

- Do I feel anxious when the client gets emotional?
- Do I feel pressure to ask the "right" question?
- Do I subtly steer the conversation toward what feels comfortable or useful?

These are moments when our presence slips, when we become *doers* instead of *holders*. But the moment we become aware, we have the power to return. To drop back into the center.

This form of presence is powerful for leaders too. When you're leading a team, a project, or a mission, you are constantly holding space, for doubt, for vision, for conflict. Detachment from outcome allows clarity. It enables you to create psychological safety even in ambiguity.

When you model this, your team learns to stay grounded amid storms. That's leadership by presence and not by force.

## The Energy of Emotional Intelligence: Without the Framework

I prefer not to speak of emotional intelligence in terms of quadrants and competencies here. Instead, I want you to *feel* it in the room.

You've been in conversations where the energy felt safe. Where the other person was fully present. You weren't being judged. You weren't being fixed. You were simply being received.

That's emotional intelligence in its purest form.

- The coach or leader is *self-aware* enough to know what they're bringing into the space, whether it's calm, tension, or agenda.
- They're *regulated* enough to stay steady even when the conversation gets uncomfortable.
- They're *attuned* enough to sense what's unspoken.
- And they're *generous* enough to stay curious rather than react.

It doesn't need a framework.
It just needs practice.
It lives in *presence*.

## Presence: A Relational Field of Resonance

Presence is often described as stillness, but in coaching mastery, presence is dynamic. It is not passive; it breathes, responds, holds, and stretches. It is both container and catalyst. Presence is not a fixed state; it is an energetic field; a finely tuned resonance between the coach and the client.

This resonance is born from a deeper kind of listening; *deep listening* that includes what the client says, but how they say it, what they don't say, and what their pauses, breath, tone, and rhythm reveal. The coach, when fully present, doesn't simply *hear* the client; they *receive* them.

Neuroscience shows us that when we attune to others with openness and calm curiosity, mirror neurons activate, creating what Daniel Siegel calls "interpersonal resonance." In this field, safety is not spoken; it is *felt*. Emotional co-regulation, grounded in presence, enables the client to feel safe enough to go deeper, trust more fully, and access layers of truth that the conscious mind often guards.

This level of presence is rooted in empathy; but empathy that is not merely emotional mirroring. It is grounded in a silent message: *I am with you, I believe in your capacity, and I don't need to rescue you*. Presence is not a soft cushion that shields clients from discomfort. It is a courageous stance that allows us to hold space when a client meets their own resistance, pain, or power.

True presence also draws from intuition: the coach's ability to sense what is beneath the words. Not guesswork, not analysis, but a quiet inner listening. Intuition guides the coach to offer questions or reflections that feel uncannily accurate, often opening a doorway the client hadn't seen before.

## The Hidden Strength of Vulnerability and Authenticity

This quality of presence cannot be cultivated through technique alone. It requires *vulnerability*; the coach's willingness to be emotionally available, to show up authentically, without the armor of expertise. Vulnerability allows the coach to feel, to risk being impacted, and to model the emotional openness that invites the client into their own authenticity.

The coach, in this space, does not pretend to have it all figured out. They are *authentic*; willing to be human, real, and attuned. Their emotional availability is a modelling of wholeness, not a breakdown of boundaries, but. By showing that it is safe to feel, to falter, and to be fully oneself, the coach becomes not just a facilitator of change, but a mirror of possibility.

Emotional exposure, in this context, is sacred. It's what allows a client to cry for the first time in a decade, to laugh freely after months of numbness, or to say, "I've never told anyone this before…" These moments don't come because of the brilliance of a question—they come because of the bravery of presence.

And presence, when held with consistency, becomes a relational anchor. Clients learn they are safe not only in a single session, but across time. This consistent energy creates the emotional scaffolding for transformation.

## Silence as an Intervention

Transformation rarely comes from brilliant monologues. It comes from the courage to hold silence. We often think of silence as empty. But in coaching, silence is data. It's reflection. It's integration.

It's the moment when the client hears their own truth rise from within.

When you are present, and I mean, truly present, you don't rush to fill the gap. You honor it. You breathe with it. You allow the discomfort to deepen into insight.

*Insight doesn't need to be delivered. It needs to be allowed.* That's what silence does. It allows.

## Case Study: The Power of Holding Space

Context
Kate, a senior operations leader in a Fortune 100 company, came into the session with clear goals. Her team had just missed a crucial project deadline. She spoke fast, brows furrowed, voice clipped.

*"I need to course-correct. What am I missing in how I lead?"*

Intervention
I could have jumped in with frameworks or powerful questions. But I sensed urgency layered over shame.

So I invited a pause.

*"Would it serve you if we just took a breath together? Not to solve, just to settle."*

We inhaled for four counts, exhaled for six. I matched her rhythm. No words. Just breathing.

Her shoulders lowered. Her eyes welled up.

*"I'm terrified they'll think I'm not strong enough,"* she whispered.

Silence followed. Thirty seconds. Then another ten. I didn't fill it. I stayed present, not rescuing, not nudging, just being.

What emerged next was not about strategy. It was about her relationship with vulnerability, her inherited beliefs about leadership, and a moment from childhood when failure meant disapproval.

Outcome
We worked over the next few sessions to redefine strength; not as stoicism, but as openness. At her next team meeting, Kate shared the missed deadline as a learning moment, inviting input. Engagement went up. Trust deepened. But more than that, she began to show up differently; with less armor and more alignment.

Reflection
That transformation didn't begin with a model. It began with presence. With my detachment from needing a "useful" session. I was involved, but not entangled. And that gave her space to find herself.

## What Gets in the Way of Presence

Presence seems simple, but it's easily disrupted. Here are common blockers:

| Blocker | What it feels like | What helps |
|---|---|---|
| **Performance pressure** | "This session has to go somewhere." | Let go of the outcome. Breathe. Trust that insight unfolds in its own time. |
| **Mental rehearsal** | Planning your next question while they speak | Come back to breath. Tune into the client's tone, not just content. |
| **Over-empathy** | You absorb the client's pain | Anchor yourself. Say silently: "This is theirs. I can witness without taking it in." |
| **Fatigue or distraction** | Numbness, zoning out | Pause. Notice your body. Feel your feet. Return gently. |

## Practices to Deepen Presence (for Coaches & Leaders)

1. Arrival Ritual (1 min before any conversation)
   Ask yourself:
   - What am I feeling right now?
   - What might I need to release to be fully here?
2. The Breath Anchor (in-session)
   3:6 breath cycle (inhale for 3, exhale for 6) during long client stories or intense emotion. Creates co-regulation.
3. Post-Session Reflection

- o Where was I most present?
- o When did I lose it?
- o What helped me return?

4. Energy Journaling
   Note conversations (inside or outside coaching) where presence shifted the dynamic. What enabled it?

5. Practice Detachment
   Before entering a session or a difficult meeting, say:
   *"I trust the process. I am here to hold—not to fix."*

## For Leaders: Presence is Strategic

Presence isn't just for coaches. It's one of the most underused tools in leadership.

A present leader:

- Builds trust faster than a charismatic one.
- Creates safety without needing to say "You're safe."
- Inspires authenticity by modelling it, not demanding it.
- Makes better decisions because they're not reacting, they're responding.

As a leader, your presence is your culture.
The way you enter a room sets the tone.
The way you listen changes what others say.
The way you pause gives others permission to think, reflect, and show up real.

Reflective Questions

- When in your life or leadership do you find yourself attached to outcome?
- What does "involved but not entangled" feel like in your body?
- How can you build a practice of detachment without disengagement?

- When have you been the recipient of deep presence? What shifted?

## The Campfire

Imagine coaching, or leadership, as sitting beside a quiet campfire. The client or team member sits across from you. The stars above watch silently. You don't stoke the flames to impress. You don't point out constellations to prove insight.

You simply tend the fire, quietly, steadily–with the kind of attention that says:

*You are safe here.*
*You are seen.*
*You are enough.*

And in that presence, something awakens. The invisible becomes visible. And the real work begins.

## The Quiet Power of Metaphors

*Where Science, Soul, and Insight Converge*

"You don't need to explain everything. Sometimes, a metaphor lights the lamp; and the whole room shifts."

Metaphors are not just language. They are portals. They speak the native tongue of the subconscious: fluid, symbolic, and resonant with truth we haven't yet found words for. I believe that in coaching, metaphors don't just decorate the conversation or describe an experience: they enhance and deepen it and transform it.

Here's why they matter—and how they work.

**Metaphors Light Up More Than Words**

Modern neuroscience confirms what wise coaches have long sensed: When someone hears a metaphor, their brain lights up in multiple regions; for language, for sensation, memory, and feeling. This is why a metaphor doesn't just clarify; it *lands*. It enters the nervous system like a coded message that the body understands before the mind catches up.

We could say that a metaphor is a shortcut to insight because it speaks in symbols, not scripts. Even more gently, metaphors take the cognitive load off & move, both client and coach into a zone of being; a slower, deeper frequency where emotional and spiritual intelligence can rise to the surface. Where meaning is not manufactured; but discovered.

Metaphors are an integral, impactful part of a coaching conversation as they ensure 'Safety Without Force'. Consider this:

Some emotions are too raw to name.
But a client can say, *"It's like I'm under a heavy wool blanket,"*
and suddenly, there's space.
The metaphor becomes a soft buffer. A safe container.
The feeling is honored; but the client is not engulfed.

This is emotional intelligence in action:
knowing emotions, and holding them wisely.

And this is spiritual intelligence, too:
Trusting that the metaphor did not arrive by accident.
That the image holds medicine.
That the client already holds the key.

## The Coach as Metaphor-Maker

Clients often arrive tangled in logic, analysis, or self-doubt. A well-placed metaphor can slice through all of that in an instant.

As a coach, your ability to offer a living metaphor at the right moment, with the right energy, can shift the entire field of the conversation.

You might reflect:

- "It feels like you're running uphill with a backpack full of bricks."
- "Sounds like your values are standing at a locked door, waiting to be let in."
- "Could it be that your inner voice is whispering through a closed window?"

These are not clever lines. They are precision tools of insight. They speak directly to the part of the client that already knows; but couldn't access until now.

Sometimes, the metaphor lands and the client goes silent.
That's the moment. The click. The deep exhale.
This is not a miracle because you were wise. It's the impact of being *aligned*, present enough to say what their soul was already aching to hear.

A well-offered metaphor doesn't explain.
It *reveals.*

## When the Image is the Intervention

Questions are powerful. And metaphors - only spoken about as a 'good to use'.

The reality is that they often do more in a single sentence than a series of well-sequenced inquiries. That's because they bypass resistance and soften defensiveness. They allow the client to see themselves, from just enough distance to witness, rather than relive.

This is why metaphor belongs not only in reflection, but in intervention.

A metaphor mirrored by the coach, or gently offered as an insight, can *connect all the wires* in the client's system.

The emotional. The logical. The somatic. The sacred.

And when that happens, it's not just a spark.
It's a 1000-watt light in the client's head and heart!

This Is Emotional and Spiritual Intelligence in Action.

A metaphor is not just a mental model. It is a felt experience. When offered with empathy, precision, and presence, it evokes emotional resonance and spiritual remembering.

Emotional Intelligence allows you to sense when a metaphor is needed. Spiritual Intelligence guides you to choose one that honors something deeper.

You're not pushing insight. You're *inviting emergence.*

Throughout this book, you've walked through metaphors
still ponds, inner storms, sacred silences, unseen fires.
They were never decoration. They were practice.

*To coach the invisible, we must speak its language.*
*And metaphor is that language.*

So listen for them. Offer them. Trust them.
Sometimes, one line, a single symbol magically shifts the ground beneath a client's story.
And that's when the real work begins.

*Metaphors are the invisible thread that weaves insight into being.*

# Chapter 6: Coaching Through Past Emotional Blocks and Inner Wounds

***"The cave you fear to enter holds the treasure you seek."*** - *Joseph Campbell*

Growth doesn't begin with ambition, it begins with courage. Not the loud kind that makes headlines, but the quiet, trembling courage to turn inwards and face the parts of ourselves we've kept hidden. Coaching that truly transforms does not just help clients manage time, change careers, or lead better—it helps them reclaim the parts of themselves frozen in time by emotional pain.

## The Armor We Wear

Each of us walks through life wearing invisible armor. It looks like confidence, people-pleasing, perfectionism, hyper-independence, or control. But underneath lies something much more tender: a hurt, an unmet need, a fear that formed when we were too young to understand it and too unequipped to process it.

Coaches often meet clients at the level of goals, but transformation begins when we gently guide them beneath the armor. Not to fix, but to witness. Not to analyze, but to allow. The most powerful shifts occur when clients feel safe enough to touch the pain that has long been denied; and in that sacred space, something begins to loosen.

## The Unconscious Mind and Emotional Imprints

The unconscious mind is not just a repository of forgotten memories; it is a living, breathing storehouse of beliefs, emotional patterns, and protective strategies built over years. Neuroscience tells us that more than 90% of our decisions and behaviors are driven not by rational thought, but by unconscious conditioning.

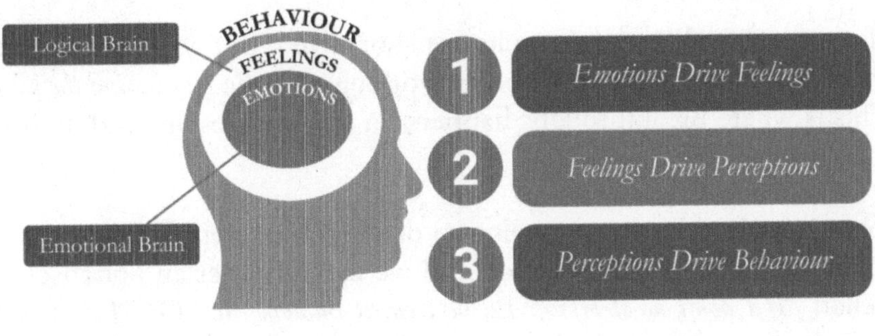


**Relationship between Emotions and Behaviour**

These imprints are formed early, often through emotionally significant events; some obvious, like trauma or neglect, and others more subtle: a teacher's shaming remark, a parent's withdrawn affection, or cultural messages around worth and success.

The emotional brain, centered around the amygdala, hippocampus, and limbic structures–remembers feelings more than facts. So while the conscious mind may forget the details, the body remembers. The client may say, "*I don't know why I react this way*," but their nervous system knows exactly why.

This is where coaching becomes both art and healing practice. When we learn to decode emotional patterns not as flaws but as protective adaptations, we can gently help the client meet themselves with compassion rather than judgment.

## The Identity Iceberg: Coaching Below the Surface

I often return to the Identity Iceberg metaphor while working with clients. At the top of the iceberg's visible tip, are behaviors: the goals, actions, and words clients bring into the coaching room. Just beneath are thoughts and feelings. And deeper still, often hidden even from the client; lie values, identity beliefs, unconscious patterns, and emotional wounds.

If we coach only the tip, results are short-lived. But when we explore the depth of the iceberg, we begin working with the *why behind the what.* This is where breakthroughs happen; in terms of results, and in how the client sees themselves.

For example, a leader struggling to delegate may not just have a time management issue. Dig deeper, and we may uncover an unconscious belief: *"If I don't do it myself, I'll be seen as incompetent."* Or *"I need to be indispensable to feel valuable."*

Such beliefs are rarely born in boardrooms; they are echoes from childhood, shaped by environments where love or acceptance was conditional.

## The Power of Vulnerability in Unfreezing the Iceberg

Emotional patterns that shape our beliefs and behaviors often live beneath the surface: unspoken, unnamed, untouched. These invisible layers, much like the submerged portion of an iceberg, are not hidden due to malice or denial. They are shielded by old conditioning, fear of judgment, or an unconscious belief that some parts of us are not acceptable.

Vulnerability begins to melt these frozen layers. It is the inner permission to feel what we feel without filtering it for approval. It invites us to step into the discomfort of being seen as we truly are.

When a client allows even a sliver of real emotion to surface: shame, sadness, longing, hope; it creates a crack in the emotional armor. That crack is where insight enters. And it rarely happens in response to advice or intellectual reframing. It happens when the client feels safe enough to reveal what has long remained hidden. Vulnerability, when held gently, becomes the gateway to release.

Authenticity deepens this work. When the client no longer performs for approval, and the coach no longer performs for impact, a different kind of conversation begins. There is no script in authenticity. There is only presence. Real presence. And in that space, something begins to soften. The walls don't collapse, but they become permeable.

Sometimes, the first act of courage is to say, 'I don't know.' Or, 'I'm afraid to feel this.' Or, 'I thought I had healed this already.' These moments signal not weakness, but readiness. The readiness to meet oneself at a deeper level.

## Courage in Direct Feedback

One of the most respectful acts in coaching is the willingness to speak to what is present, yet unspoken. Direct feedback, when rooted in care, presence, and clarity; can surface blind spots that the client has been circling for years. Not as confrontation, but as illumination.

This kind of feedback does not land as judgment. It lands as insight. It sounds like: 'I notice you shifted your tone when we touched that topic: what's happening for you there?' or 'You just said something powerful, then immediately laughed: do you sense what you're protecting in that moment?'

These invitations are not about pointing out flaws. They are about naming patterns that ask to be witnessed. The courage lies in offering the mirror, even when what it reflects might stir discomfort. And the respect lies in trusting that the client can hold that reflection with their own strength.

Direct communication, when used with discernment, becomes a scalpel that gently reveals what emotion alone cannot access. It helps bring language to sensations, precision to intuition, and clarity to confusion.

And in the presence of that clarity, the client can choose—with agency and awareness—how they want to shift. Not because the coach told them to. But because they finally saw it for themselves.

## Emotional Safety: The Foundation of Deep Coaching

Creating emotional safety is not optional when working at this level. It is the precondition. Clients do not reveal their inner world unless they feel deeply seen, heard, and held without judgment.

Presence becomes our greatest tool here. When a coach brings full presence; free from agenda, analysis, or fixing, a space opens. In that space, the client can lower their guard. They may touch sadness, shame, fear, or rage that has been waiting to be witnessed for decades.

This witnessing, without trying to change the emotion, is itself a healing act.

Neuroscience supports this: when emotions are named and validated, the amygdala reduces its threat response, and the prefrontal cortex re-engages, allowing for greater reflection and choice.

Sometimes, clients cry for the first time in years. Not because we triggered it, but because we made it *safe* enough for the dam to break.

## Cultural Sensitivity in Emotional Work

Emotional expression carries cultural codes. In some cultures, vulnerability signals strength; in others, it may feel exposing or even disrespectful. Safety, therefore, can never be assumed, it must be *co-created.* Curiosity about the client's cultural lens, and humility about our own, ensures that honoring emotions never becomes an imposing of them.

**Cultural Sensitivity: Emotional Expression Is Not Universal**

Emotional suppression is not only a personal defense, it is often a collective inheritance.

Across geographies, emotional expression is governed by invisible yet deeply entrenched cultural codes. In some societies, vulnerability is seen as strength; in others, it may be equated with weakness, dishonor, or disobedience. Anger may be sacred in one context and shameful in another. Even joy, when expressed too freely, can invite envy or judgment in environments shaped by scarcity, trauma, or colonial legacies.

Gender, caste, race, religion, and class all influence what we are permitted to feel; and more crucially, what we are permitted to *show*.

In our global coaching practice, this calls for more than empathy. It demands *cultural humility*. a willingness to recognize that emotional landscapes are shaped by generational stories, systemic oppression, and the psychological aftermath of belonging to marginalized or colonized groups. What looks like 'emotional distance' or 'lack of self-awareness' may, in fact, be the result of centuries of social conditioning.

We must explore:

- Whose emotions have been silenced?
- Whose safety depends on emotional restraint?
- Whose pain is normalized, and whose is pathologized?

In honoring emotional diversity, we open doors to deeper safety. When we hold space not only for the individual but for the cultural and historical context that shaped them, healing becomes a form of social justice.

This is not an add-on to coaching. It is at the very heart of ethical, inclusive, and transformative practice.

In these spaces, coaching becomes a quiet act of witnessing. Cultural awareness sharpens the lens: what appears like hesitation may be protection; what sounds like resistance may be inherited reverence. The coach's role is not to interpret, but to inquire gently—holding both respect and truth in the same breath.

Courage also shows up in the coach. The courage to offer a reflection that risks discomfort. The courage to stay steady when emotion surges. The courage to trust the client's process even when no clear outcome is yet in sight.

By integrating these dimensions—inner qualities, reflection practices, emotional mapping—we begin to coach not only toward outcomes, but toward alignment. This is what makes transformation sustainable. The client doesn't just achieve a result. They become someone more fully themselves.

**Invisible Wounds: Across the World**

*Emotional barriers are universal, yet healing is deeply personal and culturally shaped.*

## Emotional Mastery Through the 4 A's

When emotional pain surfaces, the client often feels overwhelmed or confused. A simple yet profound tool to guide them through this terrain is the 4 A's of Emotional Mastery:

1. Awareness: Recognizing and naming the emotion
2. Acceptance: Allowing the emotion to be without resistance
3. Articulation: Giving voice to the need or belief behind it
4. Action: Choosing a conscious response instead of a reactive one

### *The Mask of Duty*

*A senior executive in a Japanese multinational, Hiroshi was known for his stoic leadership and unshakeable calm. In coaching, he spoke of "gaman"; the cultural value of enduring hardship without complaint. Though he was respected, his team found him emotionally distant. It was only when his coach gently explored the cost of constant emotional suppression that Hiroshi shared, for the first time, the loneliness he had carried since his father's death at age 12, a grief never expressed, only endured. That single session, held with deep presence and cultural respect, opened a door to more authentic connection; with himself and his team.*

### *Veiled Strength*

*Layla, a successful entrepreneur from the UAE, entered coaching for business clarity, but her voice was guarded, her language always composed. Over time, the coach noticed her tendency to deflect emotions with achievements. In a quiet moment, when trust had deepened, Layla confided that as the eldest daughter, she had been raised to be "the pillar"—strong, silent, always responsible. Emotions were seen as indulgence, not leadership. With compassion and cultural sensitivity, the coach invited her to explore what it meant to lead from wholeness, not perfection. The permission to feel, without judgment, became Layla's turning point in redefining power not as control, but as integration.*

For example, a client feeling unexplained anxiety before presentations may uncover a belief: *"If I mess up, I'll be humiliated like that time in school."* Through awareness and articulation, they can see it's an old wound—not a present danger. From there, we can coach them toward aligned action—not from fear, but from choice.

## The Role of the Coach

Coaching at this level is not therapy, yet it touches the therapeutic. The distinction lies in the intention: we do not diagnose or treat, but we evoke awareness and presence that allows natural healing to unfold.

We never ever approach a conversation with the mindset or intention to fix the client. We are here to support the client reconnect with the wholeness that was never lost, only forgotten. When they meet their younger self with kindness, when they allow tears to fall without shame, when they rewrite old beliefs with empowered truths: that's when the shift becomes lasting.

Healing is not a detour from coaching or performance. It is the gateway to it. A leader who is no longer driven by unresolved fears leads with greater clarity. A professional who no longer carries the weight of proving their worth creates from a place of joy and freedom.

Inner Healing = Sustainable Growth

Surface-level change is fast and fleeting. Inner transformation is slower; but it sticks. When a client works through their emotional barriers, they achieve better results *and* they experience perceptible inner shifts. More self-aware. More resilient. More emotionally intelligent. They begin to trust their own wisdom. They show up more authentically in teams, relationships, and leadership.

This is not just coaching for success. It is coaching for wholeness; because when wholeness is restored, success becomes a by-product.

## Case Study: Healing the Invisible Wounds

Client: Arend, Senior Director in a multinational tech firm

Presenting Issue: *"I need help managing conflict with my new team. I find myself shutting down or overreacting when challenged."*

At first glance, this seemed like a typical leadership development issue; conflict resolution, communication skills, perhaps some assertiveness training. As we explored, something deeper emerged.

Arend's emotional response to conflict was disproportionate to the situation. A casual disagreement would leave him feeling anxious or defensive for hours. When asked about his earliest memory of conflict, he hesitated. Then quietly said, "My father would explode in anger. I learned to disappear."

This childhood imprint had shaped his adult behavior. In the workplace, any challenge was perceived, not consciously, but viscerally, as a threat to his safety.

Together, we applied the 4 A's:

- Awareness: Recognizing that his shutdown response was not a flaw but a survival mechanism.
- Acceptance: Allowing himself to feel the fear, without trying to push it away.
- Articulation: Naming the belief: *"If I speak up, I'll be attacked."*
- Action: Practicing safe, small moments of assertiveness in team settings, gradually expanding his capacity.

Over several sessions, something shifted. He no longer saw conflict as dangerous, but as data. He began to hold his ground, not with aggression, but calm confidence.

Arend's transformation wasn't just about team performance. He reported sleeping better, connecting more deeply with his teenage son, and most touchingly, writing a letter to his father, never sent, but fully felt.

This is the power of emotional healing. It ripples into every part of life.

## We Hear the Boiling Pot; But Stay in the Present

As coaches, we often encounter clients who are sitting on a boiling pot of emotions. Anger, sadness, shame, fear: bubbling just beneath the surface of their narratives. These emotions may originate from the past, but our role is not to take them back there. We are not historians of pain. We are facilitators of growth.

We do not regress or revisit the past to fix it. Instead, we:

- Acknowledge what's present,
- We listen deeply, and

- We support the client in moving forward; anchored in the here and now.

Emotional healing through coaching is not about reliving the wound; it's about meeting the emotion that's alive in this moment, and offering it a new response.

Where therapy might explore *why* the pain started, coaching holds space for *what* wants to emerge now. We help the client make sense of their present patterns and choose how they want to show up going forward.

We might say:

*"I hear how strongly this situation has impacted you. Let's explore what this emotion might be inviting you to pay attention to in your current journey."*

In doing so, we honor the client's story without making the story the destination. We focus on growth, not excavation. On insight, not investigation.

### A Note to the Coach

*There will be moments when your client's pain activates your own. You may feel helpless, uncertain, or moved to tears. Navigate that surge of emotion, manage it. That is presence, not failure. Coaching the invisible requires inner spaciousness. Keep tending to your own growth so you can stay soft and steady within theirs. Transformation, yours and theirs—unfolds in that field of shared humanity.*

### What Clients Say but Don't Say: Words That Whisper The Wound

- "I don't get emotional; I just move on."
- "I've always been the strong one."
- "That's just how things were back then."
- "Let's not go into the past, I'm fine now."

### Emotional Timeline vs. Intellectual Timeline

| Intellectual Timeline | Emotional Timeline |
|---|---|
| "I've forgiven them." | Still carries distrust in relationships |
| "I've made peace with the past." | Avoids intimacy or conflict |
| "That happened 20 years ago." | Nervous system still hypervigilant |

### The Role of the Body in Emotional Release

Emotions are not just "felt", they are stored. The nervous system, fascia, breath, and gut all carry emotional memory. For sustainable growth, coaching interventions must allow the body to speak: through breathwork, somatic cues, and mindfulness. Holding space for stillness, shaking, or silence can allow a breakthrough that no amount of talking can unlock.

## Reflect and Integrate

Use the questions below to anchor the chapter's insights in your own experience; whether you are a coach, leader, or lifelong learner:

1. *Where do I notice emotional patterns repeating, either in my clients, my team, or myself?*
2. *What part of my own story still seeks simple acknowledgement, no excavation, just gentle naming?*
3. *How do I create emotional safety when someone cannot yet name what they feel?*
4. *Which emotion am I least comfortable witnessing in others, and what might that reveal about my own journey?*
5. *When protecting feels like personality, how can I invite curiosity instead of judgment?*

Pause with each question. Journal, breathe, or discuss with a peer coach. Insight is the first step; integration is the journey.

## Coach's Mirror: Pause and Witness

Take a breath here.

As a coach, how often do you pause, to listen to your client and to witness your own reactions, your own subtle armors?

You've likely felt it; the urge to steer the conversation away from tears, or the quick fix that saves the session from discomfort. These are not flaws. They are human instincts. But what if the moment you feel most unsure… is the very moment you're being invited into deeper presence?

In that space, your silence can be more healing than strategy. Your stillness, more powerful than tools. The client does not need you to be fearless; they need you to be real, grounded, and available to witness their unseen wounds without flinching.

This is not about doing more. It is about being more.

And that is the quiet brilliance of our work.

To coach someone through their emotional barriers is a sacred act. We become witnesses to their pain, midwives to their breakthroughs, and custodians of their transformation. But we must tread gently. This is not about digging up wounds, it is about offering light to places that have long been in shadow.

In every emotionally charged moment, we must ask ourselves:

*Can I hold this without needing to fix it?*
*Can I meet their pain without fear or urgency?*
*Can I trust the client's wholeness, even when they cannot see it yet?*

When we answer yes to these questions, we do more than coach. We heal, one conversation at a time.

This is about 'Coaching the Intangible to Achieve or Manifest the Tangible'.

# Part Three

# Coaching the Whole Self – The Inward Journey

The general understanding is that the emotional and the spiritual are different and distinct in nature but I believe that they do intersect in a very profound manner.

The emotional & spiritual aspects are interdependent. How does it start? The entire concept starts with understanding the self, others, & the world around us. I believe emotions drive people, and people drive performance. Emotions are that spectrum of feelings that respond to internal & external stimuli. They are the signals that communicate our internal state & determine our thoughts, decisions, & actions. Spirituality encompasses a deep sense of connection to oneself. It is about seeking meaning, purpose & transcendence beyond the material & tangible realm. Coaching these two aspects results in effective achievement of tangible goals.

As we journey through emotional awareness and mastery, we begin to see emotions not merely as patterns to manage, but as doorways to something deeper. Once the noise of reactivity quietens, a gentle voice emerges from within, the voice of inner wisdom.

This is where the coaching journey evolves from insight to inner sight. Emotional intelligence helps us navigate our responses to the world; spiritual intelligence helps us understand our place in it. It invites coaches and clients alike to go beyond strategies and outcomes, into the realm of meaning, presence, and deep alignment.

# Chapter 7: Coaching with Inner Wisdom

***"Within you, there is a stillness and sanctuary to which you can retreat at any time and be yourself."*** - *Hermann Hesse*

## The Intersection of Coaching & Spirituality

There is a quiet intelligence within each of us. There is a silent companion that walks with us through every decision, every crossroad, and every transformation. It does not shout, demand, or compete. It whispers. It nudges. It invites. This is the voice of inner wisdom, the stillness beneath the noise, the clarity behind confusion. It offers a deeper knowing, not from books or advice, but from the quiet center within. And in coaching, it is perhaps our most powerful and most underutilized guide.

Coaching is often seen as a process of asking powerful questions, clarifying goals, and building accountability. In the coaching space, we often meet clients at a crossroads: successful but unfulfilled, busy but lost, capable but disconnected.

But beyond the visible arc of the conversation lies an invisible current, a field of presence, intuition, energy, and meaning. This is where spiritual intelligence enters. This is where we begin coaching the whole person. Let's explore the intersection of coaching and spirituality as an invitation into higher consciousness and not as a religious or dogmatic concept. It is about accessing wisdom that transcends logic, holding space for transformation that originates from the soul. Beneath the surface of goals and action plans, they seek something more, a sense of purpose, of meaning, of wholeness.

**Coaching Beyond Belief, Into Being**

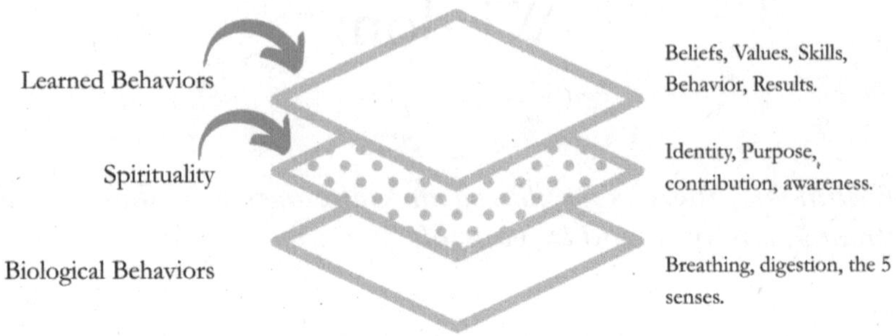


Coaching brings us into intimate contact with a client's goals, challenges, and inner world. But every so often, beneath the story they're telling, we hear something else.

A hesitation.
A sigh.
A shift in tone.
A sentence that carries more weight than the words themselves.

And in that moment, something in us pauses. We sense that the conversation is brushing against a deeper truth; something the client hasn't fully named, but already knows. That's the space where inner wisdom begins to emerge.

This wisdom doesn't sound like a strategy. It doesn't arrive in neat steps or frameworks. It's quieter. More grounded. It shows up in the way someone suddenly sits up straighter, or how they soften when they speak about something meaningful.

Inner wisdom is not a concept. It's an experience, one that both the coach and client can feel when the space is open enough to hold it.

Many clients come to coaching with questions about what to do, how to lead, or where to go next. Beneath those questions is often something more fundamental:

- *What truly matters to me?*
- *What do I want my life to stand for?*
- *What am I being called toward that I haven't yet found the courage to follow?*

These are not philosophical diversions. They are the real questions that give direction to all the others.

And yet, they don't always appear upfront. Most clients don't come into a session saying, "I want to connect with my inner wisdom." They come with surface goals — productivity, team dynamics, decision-making, balance. It's only when the coaching space feels safe, respectful, and unhurried that the deeper questions start to rise.

As coaches, we must learn to recognize those moments. And rather than rushing past them, we pause. We become curious. We invite the client to listen inward; not to us, to themselves. In a world full of noise, this may be one of the most profound things we can offer: *The space to hear one's own voice again.*

This part of 'Coaching the Intangible' invites you to explore coaching as a behavioral & emotional process, and as a spiritual journey; where both coach and client meet in a space of stillness, authenticity, and higher truth.

## Spirituality in Coaching: Beyond Belief, Into Being

When we speak of "inner wisdom," many people immediately associate it with spirituality. But let's pause here to define spirituality, and to broaden it.

Coaching is a very structured approach to spirituality. because it encourages looking inward and within.

Spirituality, as it shows up in coaching, isn't about religion. It's not about doctrine, rituals, or sacred texts, unless that's where a client personally finds their meaning. Instead, it's about helping people access something deeper than thought. A knowing. A felt sense of connectedness to self, others, and the world.

Some call it soul.
Others call it higher self, source, intuition, or simply presence.
Whatever the term, it's the part of a person that seeks alignment with truth and measurable, tangible productivity.

In the coaching room, spirituality may show up in the form of:

- A longing to live with purpose
- A desire to contribute to something larger than oneself
- An awareness that external success no longer feels fulfilling
- A sudden grief that has no clear reason; only depth
- A moment of stillness that arrives in silence

These moments are sacred in their capacity to transform. When clients touch this place, something shifts. The clutter of options and overthinking falls away, and what remains is a clarity that feels deeply personal and yet universally human.

As coaches, we are not here to preach. We're not gurus, guides, or wise sages. We're simply present. And in our presence, we model something rare: the *courage* to sit with what is unseen but deeply felt. It does need courage to coach at this level as it may be beyond the coach's own comfort level; unaware of navigating this unseen, intangible territory.

Sometimes, the most profound coaching tool is a meaningful pause. It may be quiet "hmm…" It's honoring the space that opens when a client touches something true.

When spirituality becomes part of the coaching conversation; organically, not forced, we begin coaching the *whole* person. Not just the thinker. Not just the achiever. But the individual who is seeking meaning, connection, and wholeness.

And that's what coaching the inner self is about:
*Peeling away layers - not adding more..*
So that what remains is not a new identity; but an authentic one.

To coach with inner wisdom involves recognizing that each client has an inner compass; a deep knowing that is often buried under layers of conditioning, fear, and societal expectations. Spirituality, in this context, is about evoking the 'why' at the next level and drawing out what is already present but invisible.

This could include:

- Meaning: Helping the client ask, *Why does this matter to me?*
- Purpose: Supporting them in discovering what they are truly here for.
- Consciousness: Expanding their awareness beyond the immediate, into the timeless.

Let's begin by untying spirituality from religion.

Spiritual intelligence is not about following rituals or subscribing to belief systems. In the coaching space, it's not about introducing prayers or sacred texts. Rather, it is about evoking inner truth, helping the client access a sense of connection; with themselves, with others, with life itself.

In simple terms:

- Emotional intelligence asks: *How do I feel, and how do I manage those feelings?*
- Spiritual intelligence asks: *Why am I here? What is truly important? What deeper truth is calling me forward?*

Clients may not use the word "spiritual," but they come seeking goals in this area. It may manifest as:

- "I've achieved everything, but I still feel empty."
- "I want to do something that matters."

- "I'm tired of pretending to be someone I'm not."
- "I need to find myself again."

These aren't logistical problems. They are *soul signals*. Coaching at this level requires us to listen beyond the words; to sense the longing beneath the goal, the calling beneath the complaint.

To listen for and coach the soul signals, we must hold space for both the outer and inner journey, by trusting that the wisdom already exists within the client.

## Blending Inner Traditions with Modern Practice

As coaches deepen into the realm of spiritual intelligence, a different kind of guidance begins to emerge; one that is not purely cognitive or emotional, but quietly intuitive. This guidance draws strength from stillness, from silence, from something deeper than problem-solving. At this level, transformation is no longer about doing more. It is about becoming more whole.

The wisdom traditions of the East offer valuable pathways into this dimension of coaching. Practices like mindfulness, meditation, contemplation, and presence are not tools to be used—they are states to be inhabited. These ancient disciplines remind us that clarity often arises not through analysis, but through spaciousness. That truth surfaces when there is enough quiet to hear it. That presence itself is transformative.

When coaching integrates Eastern principles, it invites the client into an inner alignment that is often bypassed in conventional goal-driven models. The inquiry shifts from 'What should I do?' to 'Who am I becoming?' From 'What am I solving?' to 'What am I sensing?' In this space, the coaching process becomes less about pushing forward and more about arriving fully.

Presence, in this tradition, is not just attentiveness. It is a field of awareness that honors the client's pace, values their silence, and holds space for the unknown. The coach becomes a companion in stillness as an expert, as a fellow traveler. This presence is not passive. It is a deep attentiveness to the client's inner world, a listening that extends beyond the ears.

These practices can be seamlessly woven into coaching without ritual or doctrine. A mindful pause before beginning. A question that arises from intuition rather than agenda. A moment of shared stillness when a client says something that shifts the air in the room. These subtle invitations allow the client to access their own wisdom; from the clarity of the soul.

## Why Inner Wisdom Matters in Coaching

Many clients are trained to analyze, decide, and act quickly. In this fast-paced world, inner wisdom is often drowned out by urgency, comparison, and noise.

Yet it is inner wisdom that:

- Offers clarity when the mind is confused
- Anchors choices in values, not just trends
- Guides clients through uncertainty and transitions
- Connects them with purpose, not just productivity

This wisdom is subtle. It doesn't always offer linear answers. It shows up as:

- A gut feeling or intuition
- A sense of resonance or dissonance
- A quiet inner yes or no
- A persistent nudge that won't go away

As coaches, we must learn to recognize this voice, both in ourselves and in our clients. And more importantly, we must create the safety and silence for it to emerge.

## Cultivating Meaning and Purpose in Coaching Conversations

Clients don't come to coaching just to solve problems.
They come because something within them is restless.

They may articulate it as confusion, a desire to change careers, a loss of motivation, or a hunger for better work-life balance. But beneath the surface, what they're really searching for is meaning.

- "Why am I doing this?"
- "What really matters now?"
- "Is this all there is?"

These are not questions the logical mind alone can answer. They come from a deeper part of the psyche, one that wants more than just outcomes.

It wants coherence.

Purpose.

Peace.

Belonging.

As coaches, we aren't here to hand out meaning or suggest what someone's purpose should be. We're here to help them listen, to tune inward until they begin to recognize the patterns of longing that have always been whispering beneath their life's noise.

One of the most powerful spiritual questions we can ask a client is:
"*What gives your life meaning?*"

In a results-driven world, this can feel like a radical detour. But it is often the doorway to true transformation.

Clients rarely arrive with this question in mind. Instead, they bring career decisions, leadership challenges, life transitions. But when we slow down and hold space, the conversation begins to deepen:

- *What does success mean to me now?*
- *What am I truly seeking?*
- *Where have I lost connection with myself?*
- *What values have I compromised?*
- *What is calling me that I'm afraid to name?*

These are not coaching techniques, they are invitations to the soul.

And yet, we must be skillful. Not every client is ready for this journey. We must pace it with presence and permission. We must read the energy in the space, and trust our intuition to know when to go deeper.

## Cultivating Meaning, Purpose, and Higher Consciousness

*Spiritual Intelligence in the Coaching Relationship*

Meaning isn't found. It's felt.

We've often been told that purpose is a goal or destination. We learn that purpose is more like a direction, a felt sense of alignment that draws people toward something more whole, more true. For some clients, this might look like creating social impact. For others, it might be simplifying their lives or deepening their relationships. For still others, it might be an inner shift that no one sees, but that changes everything.

The common thread? It makes life feel worth living.

This is why a conversation about purpose can't be rushed or checklist driven. It requires stillness. Spaciousness. And a willingness to sit with silence because sometimes the truest things show up when we stop trying to figure them out.

*Recognizing the Moment When Meaning Emerges*

There's a quiet moment in some coaching sessions; a shift in energy, a softening in the client's voice, when they touch something real. They may not have the perfect words for it. But their whole presence changes. You sense that they've moved out of analysis and into knowing.

As one client once said to me, mid-sentence:
*"I don't know why I'm crying. I just… know I have to do this."*

That moment had nothing to do with strategy.
It was the voice of her inner wisdom, and she'd finally heard it.

As coaches, we must learn to stay with such moments. Not interpret them, not move on too quickly, not fill the silence. Just stay. These are the moments that transform lives, because they realign people with something larger than themselves.

*Higher Consciousness Isn't About Lofty States, It's About Deep Presence*

The phrase "higher consciousness" can feel intimidating or abstract. But in coaching, we're not chasing enlightenment. We're inviting presence. Awareness. Inner spaciousness. In practice, this often shows up in the simplest of ways:

- A client recognizes that their need for external approval no longer serves them.
- They begin to see a difficult colleague with compassion instead of defensiveness.
- They start trusting that their inner knowing is valid, even if others don't understand it.

These are not intellectual shifts. They are perceptual shifts, subtle yet profound changes in how a client sees themselves and the world. And once these shifts occur, their decisions, actions, and relationships begin to reorganize around that expanded awareness.

This is what makes inner wisdom such a powerful compass. It doesn't just answer "what should I do?"

It reframes the question entirely into something more like:
*"Who am I now, and how do I want to live from here?"*

## Coaching Practices to Cultivate Higher Awareness

Let's be clear: we're not spiritual gurus. But we are facilitators of inner inquiry.
There are gentle yet powerful ways we can help clients access their deeper wisdom:

### Presence-based questioning

Ask questions that slow the pace and deepen reflection:
*"If you were to quiet the noise for a moment, what does your heart already know?"*
*"What feels true, not just logical or correct?"*

### Noticing somatic cues

The body often responds before the mind catches up. When a client touches something meaningful, you might notice a sigh, stillness, or tears. Naming this gently can help anchor the insight:
*"I noticed you became very quiet just now. What's happening inside?"*

### Meaning mapping

Invite the client to map moments in their life when they felt most alive or aligned. Patterns often emerge, not of activity, but of values: contribution, authenticity, freedom, connection. These become clues to purpose.

### The pause practice

When faced with a big decision, encourage the client to pause, breathe, and listen inwardly. This helps separate reactive thoughts from true inner guidance.

### Invite the sacred in their language

For some clients, "spirituality" may be tied to nature, creativity, or ancestral wisdom. Meet them where they are. Use the language they trust. The goal is not to impose beliefs but to help them connect to what is already sacred to them.

## Client Reflection Exercise

### Moments That Mattered

Ask your client to reflect and write about three moments in their life when they felt deeply fulfilled.

Then ask:

- What was present in those moments?
- What values or truths were you living from?
- What does this tell you about what really matters to you now?

The sense of purpose isn't always grand. Sometimes, it's subtle.

When we bring spiritual intelligence into the coaching process, it is not something we "do", it is who we are.

This includes:

- Presence: The ability to be fully in the moment without agenda.
- Compassionate Witnessing: Holding space without judgment, advice, or rescue.
- Deep Listening: Hearing not just what is said, but what is not said.
- Intuition: Trusting the felt sense and inner nudges during the session.
- Humility: Recognizing that the answers lie within the client, not the coach.

Coaching with spiritual intelligence is about becoming a mirror. We do not lead the client down a spiritual path. We simply reflect their own truth back to them, until they can see it clearly.

## Practices That Awaken Inner Wisdom

The following practices can be integrated into coaching sessions to help clients access their inner wisdom:

### 1. Centering & Stillness

Begin a session with a pause. Invite the client to breathe, to drop in, to feel the present moment. Even 30 seconds of silence can shift the energy dramatically.

Sample Invitation:
"*Let's take a moment to settle in. Feel your feet on the floor, take a few slow breaths, and just notice what's here for you in this moment.*"

### 2. Values Reflection

Ask the client to recall a moment in their life when they felt deeply fulfilled. *What values were being honored? What does this reveal about what truly matters to them?*

### 3. The Inner Council

Invite the client to imagine a wise inner voice: a mentor, elder, future self, or even a symbolic guide. Ask:
*"What would this wise part of you say about this situation?"*

### 4. Sacred Questions

Not every question needs an immediate answer. Some are meant to linger.

Examples:

- *"What is life inviting you to learn here?"*
- *"What truth have you been avoiding?"*
- *"If you fully trusted yourself, what would you do?"*

Let these questions echo. Sometimes, the insight arrives after the session ends.

There's a myth that purpose has to be big: start a movement, launch a foundation, change the world. However, for one of my clients, purpose looked like healing their family relationships. For another, it meant creating art again, not for recognition, but for joy.

In a world obsessed with productivity, choosing inner alignment with purpose.is a radical act. We must expand our lens, to see purpose not just as vocation, but as *vibration.* Not as one fixed path, but as an inner compass that keeps evolving as the client evolves.

This is what keeps the coaching process sacred.
Not that we have the answers, but that we walk with the client as they remember what they've always known.

## The Neuroscience of Inner Wisdom

While spirituality may feel intangible, science has begun to validate the power of inner knowing. Research into heart-brain coherence, mindfulness, and intuition shows that:

- The heart sends more signals to the brain than the brain sends to the heart, and these influence clarity and decision-making.
- Quieting the analytical mind activates the default mode network, associated with self-reflection and insight.
- Intuition is a form of rapid pattern recognition, a kind of wisdom the body stores even when the mind forgets.

In the context of coaching, these insights remind us that truth doesn't always arrive through logic. Often, it emerges when we slow down, tune in, and listen deeply.

## The Body Remembers: Somatic Intelligence in Emotional Coaching

Emotions aren't only stories we tell ourselves, they are physical experiences. The body responds long before the mind interprets. A tight jaw, a fluttering chest, a sinking belly: these are often the first signs that something within us is asking to be seen.

We often listen to the words, and some of the most valuable insights come from listening to the body. This is where somatic intelligence enters the arena: a layer of awareness that helps clients locate, understand, and eventually release the emotional patterns stored in the body.

Trauma expert Bessel van der Kolk reminds us that "the body keeps the score." Long-held stress, unprocessed grief, and even outdated belief systems leave a trace in muscle tone, breath patterns, and posture. When a client says, "I don't know why I feel stuck," their words may be true; but the body often does know.

*Practice: Name, Notice, Neutralize*

A simple, coachable somatic process:

1. **Name the sensation**
   Ask: "Where in your body do you feel that right now?"
2. **Notice its qualities**
   Is it sharp, heavy, hot, still? Movement or pressure?
3. **Neutralize by bringing breath and attention**
   Invite a few slow breaths into that area—not to fix, but to witness.

This isn't about diagnosing or analyzing the body—it's about creating space for the body to speak. Clients who access somatic cues often find breakthroughs that words alone could not reach.

Coaching often moves in subtle, nonlinear ways. But underneath the unfolding conversation, something more structured is happening—within the client's brain, body, and emotional system. By understanding this invisible flow, coaches can better attune to what stage their client may be in and offer interventions that truly land.

Here is a simplified map of the neuro-emotional arc a client often travels in a transformational coaching session:

## The Flow: From Trigger to Choice

1. **Trigger or Pattern Activation**
    - Limbic system is activated; amygdala may hijack rational thought.
    - Emotional flooding, reactivity, or confusion arises.
2. **Pause and Awareness**
    - The coach invites presence.
    - Awareness shifts from story to sensation.
3. **Breath and Regulation**
    - Client slows down, re-engages the prefrontal cortex.
    - Emotional charge begins to soften.
4. **Naming the Emotion**
    - Emotional granularity increases; meaning becomes clearer.
    - Inner coherence begins to emerge.
5. **Reframing or Insight**
    - With the prefrontal cortex online, perspective broadens.
    - Insight is no longer forced—it arises.
6. **Choice and Aligned Action**
    - Client sees options they couldn't access before.
    - New neural pathways begin forming.

This process is rarely linear, but it's helpful to know what you're holding space for. Sometimes the most important thing a coach can do is slow the moment between step 1 and step 2 to make room for awareness before the mind rushes to solve or justify.

## Cultural Sensitivity: Spirituality Across Contexts

Spiritual intelligence is not culturally neutral. The way clients relate to inner wisdom is shaped by:

- Religious or spiritual upbringing
- Cultural values and taboos
- Language and metaphors they feel safe using
- Historical experiences with authority, intuition, or belief

It's imperative that we honor these differences. Some clients may resonate with terms like "soul," "divine," or "calling." Others may prefer "intuition," "alignment," or "inner compass." What matters is not the language we use, but the truth it points to. Let the client lead in defining the terms that feel authentic and empowering.

## Case Study: Finding Purpose Beyond Profit

Name: Aditya

Age: 44-year

Profile: Founder of a highly successful fintech company in Singapore.

After scaling rapidly and achieving unicorn status, he approached coaching with a sense of burnout and emptiness.

*"I should be celebrating. But I feel numb. Disconnected. I don't know what I'm doing anymore."*

At first, the coaching focused on work-life balance, team dynamics, and re-establishing vision. But as trust deepened, the conversation shifted.

Coach: *"When was the last time you felt truly alive, not just successful?"*

Aditya recalled a community initiative his company had once supported, a financial literacy project for underserved youth in rural India.

*"That was the only time I felt… right. Like this work mattered."*

That memory became the turning point. Over the next few sessions, the coach invited him into deeper reflection:

- *What values had he abandoned in the pursuit of scale?*
- *What kind of legacy did he want to leave behind?*
- *What if profit was no longer the north star?*

The shift was internal first. Aditya began listening to his own inner wisdom; not the market, not investors. From there, tangible change followed. He restructured his company to include a purpose division, redefined success metrics, and began mentoring young entrepreneurs who wanted to build with heart.

*"I didn't need a new business plan. I needed to remember who I am."*

This is the power of coaching with inner wisdom.

*The transformation wasn't imposed, it was invoked.*

## Reflective Questions for Coaches

Before we can evoke inner wisdom in our clients, we must learn to recognize it in ourselves.

Ask yourself:

- *When do I feel most aligned with my inner truth?*
- *How do I distinguish between my ego and my intuition?*
- *Do I create space for silence in my sessions?*
- *Am I willing to let go of my plan if the client's inner voice leads us elsewhere?*

Coaching with inner wisdom requires courage. It is not always comfortable. But it is deeply, quietly transformative.

## The Coach as a Sacred Mirror

In spiritual traditions across cultures, transformation begins with reflection, not advice. In many ways, this is what the coach becomes: a sacred mirror. We reflect the client's own essence, their light, their longing, their wholeness, until they can see it for themselves.

We hold presence when they forget their worth.
We listen deeply when the world is loud.
We believe in their inner wisdom until they begin to trust it.

And in doing so, we honor the sacred role coaching can play in helping people perform better, but in helping them connect with their authentic selves.

When a client brings up career dissatisfaction or "feeling stuck," pause and ask yourself:
*Is this about goals… or is it about purpose?*
Sometimes the greatest service you can offer is helping them explore what "success" really means now, not what it meant five years ago.

After all, purpose is not something we pursue. It's something we allow.

Coaching with inner wisdom is not a technique. It is a way of being. It calls us, as coaches, to embody stillness, to trust silence, and to walk alongside our clients, perhaps holding a light to illuminate their path. on the path back to themselves.

It is, ultimately, the deepest service we can offer:
Not to give answers, but to help another listen to the wisdom they've always carried within.

# Chapter 8: Intuition in Coaching-Wisdom in Action

***"Intuition is not a hunch, it's accumulated inner data calling your attention."*** - *Inspired by Myss, Kahneman & countless wise coaches*

## The Silent Voice Within

Have you ever been in a coaching session where, despite the topic seeming straightforward, a quiet whisper in your heart said, *"This isn't really what it's about"?* You might have felt a slight tightening in your chest, an image flashing briefly through your mind, or a deep sense of "there's something more here."

That's intuition speaking.

It's not loud. It doesn't clamor for attention. It doesn't explain itself with a bullet-pointed rationale. It arrives gently, like a feather brushing across your consciousness. And if we're present enough, still enough, humble enough, we listen.

In coaching, that inner whisper can be the bridge between superficial dialogue and soul-level transformation. It is, in many ways, wisdom in action.

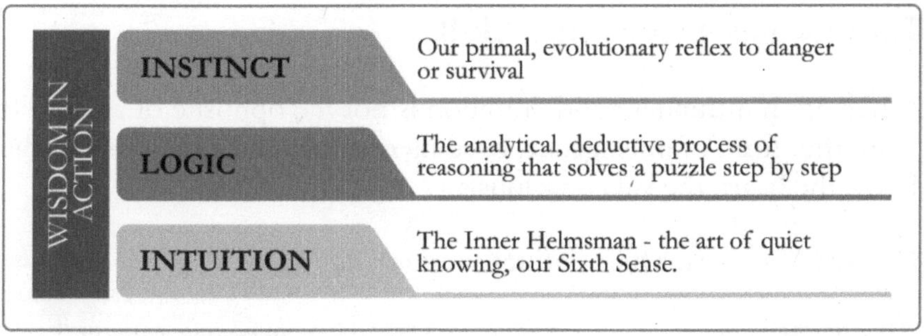


## Beyond Instinct and Logic

Let's begin by honoring what intuition is *not*. It is not instinct; our primal, evolutionary reflex to danger or survival. Nor is it logic, the analytical, deductive process of reasoning that solves a puzzle step by step.

Intuition is something more subtle.

Where instinct is primal and logic is deliberate, intuition is quiet knowing.

Imagine a seasoned coach sitting with a client. The client talks about struggling with delegation, but the coach notices the slightest quiver in the voice when the word "trust" comes up. A picture flashes in the coach's mind: the client standing alone in a crowd. The coach doesn't jump to conclusions, but the image stays. It guides the next question:

*"I'm sensing this might be more about feeling unsupported than about delegation. Would that resonate?"*

And in that moment, the client exhales, as if relieved that someone finally named the unnamed.

That is intuition. Not magic or mystery, but a natural intelligence that we all carry.

## Intuition as a Coaching Skill

While often misunderstood, intuition is not the opposite of reason. It is another form of intelligence, residing not only in the mind but in the body, the heart, the subconscious.

Carolyn Myss beautifully defines intuition as:

*"The ability to use energy data to make decisions in the immediate moment."*

We are constantly reading energy, tone, pace, posture, pauses. Intuition translates that data into insight. It is our capacity to receive information beyond logic, often through images, feelings, bodily sensations, or subtle energetic shifts.

And here's the secret:
We all have it.
We all use it.
We just don't always recognize it; or trust it. Honing into this gift would benefit every relationship , every profession.

### The Whisper Beneath the Words

In the quietest moments of a coaching conversation, when logic seems insufficient and analysis feels intrusive, another voice often rises; subtle, yet compelling. It may not arrive with clarity or data, but it pulses with knowing. That voice is intuition.

We are aware of the significance of listening deeply, fully; beyond the words our clients speak, down to the second layer of listening: to the unspoken. It is the space between the lines, the felt sense in the room, the energetic shift in a client's tone or posture. Intuition, in this realm, becomes more than a tool; it is a guide.

The question that has come up over the years is, 'how do we discern between the sacred clarity of intuition and the sneaky impostor that is cognitive bias? When does inner knowing truly serve the client, and when might it subtly serve our own narratives?

This chapter invites you into that exploration.

## Understanding Intuitive Intelligence in Coaching

Intuition is not a mystical superpower reserved for a gifted few. It is a form of intelligence, grounded in the integration of experience, emotional resonance, and subconscious pattern recognition. Neuroscientists have identified that the brain often processes information faster than our conscious mind can articulate. This means we sometimes "know" without knowing how we know.

Daniel Kahneman, in *Thinking, Fast and Slow*, referred to these two systems as System 1 (fast, intuitive) and System 2 (slow, deliberate). While System 2 is analytical and cautious, System 1 offers swift judgments based on stored patterns and emotional impressions. Both have value. But in coaching, it is System 1, our intuitive system; that often picks up the subtle clues that logic misses.

In intuitive coaching, we access this rapid, felt-sense intelligence to:

- Notice emotional undercurrents
- Ask questions that feel "guided"
- Sense what is unsaid, but deeply true
- Intervene not because of evidence, but because of resonance

At its best, intuition allows us to hold space in a way that feels divinely timed. The client feels seen, not just heard. Known, not just observed. The shift is palpable.

## Intuition vs. Bias: The Subtle Distinction

If intuition is a whisper, bias is a ventriloquist. It mimics inner knowing but often speaks from fear, assumption, or ego. It tells us, *"You've seen this before; you know what's going on."* It generalizes. It rushes. It assumes.

It follows that we must be vigilant about this. Bias wears many masks:

- Confirmation bias: Looking for signs that validate our belief about the client
- Projection: Mistaking our emotional landscape for theirs
- Cultural bias: Interpreting through our own lens without honoring theirs

While intuition arises from stillness, bias arises from noise. Particularly the noise of unexamined beliefs. Intuition feels expansive; bias feels conclusive. Intuition leaves space for the client; bias closes it.

One litmus test I often use is this:

*Does what I'm sensing evoke curiosity, or certainty?*
If it's curiosity, I lean in. If it's certainty, I pause.

## The Body as Barometer

One of the most powerful doorways to intuition is the body.

Think of how we use phrases like:

*"I had a gut feeling."*
*"My heart wasn't in it."*
*"Something didn't sit right."*

These are not poetic metaphors. They are literal sensory signals. Intuition often speaks through the body long before the mind catches up. Cultivating body-awareness allows us to *feel* into the conversation, not just hear it.

*Try this:*
Before your next session, place your attention on the soles of your feet. Ground yourself. Breathe deeply. Then, as your client speaks, notice; what shifts in your body? Do you feel tension, warmth, tingling, stillness? These are not distractions; they are *data.*

When integrated skillfully, such intuitive signals can lead to profound insights, offered with humility, curiosity, and non-attachment.

| | | |
|---|---|---|
| Hardwired, evolutionary | Learned, methodical | Emerges from presence and energy sensing |
| Reactive (e.g. fight/flight) | Step-by-step problem solving | Insight that defies linear explanation |

## Developing Your Intuitive Intelligence

If intuition is a muscle, it strengthens with practice.

You don't need to be clairvoyant. You simply need to be present. Intuition arises not in striving, but in stillness. Here are some practices to help deepen your intuitive coaching presence:

### 1. Presence before Performance

Start each session with 2–3 minutes of silence. Let go of any "agenda." Ask yourself, *"What would it mean to be fully open today?"* You're not trying to be intuitive—you're preparing to receive.

### 2. Somatic Shifts

During a session, place gentle awareness on your body. What sensations arise when the client says certain words? Where does your body feel open, where does it contract?

### 3. Metaphor Journaling

Post-session, reflect on metaphors or images that arose. These often come from the subconscious and may carry wisdom beyond logic.

### 4. The 'Sense' Statements

Practice using light, permission-based language to share intuitive insights:

- "I'm wondering if…"
- "Something in me feels like there's more beneath this…"

- "I have the sense that…"

These statements allow the client to explore rather than feel directed. You're not instructing; you're inviting.

## Tuning the Intuitive Channel

Intuition is a quiet channel, easily drowned out by noise, mental chatter, emotional attachment, performance anxiety. To hear it clearly, we must attune.

A 2021 study by Sadler-Smith & Burke suggests that *intuitive decision-making engages both the default mode network and salience network in the brain*; meaning we process intuition by toggling between past experience and in-the-moment awareness.

Like tuning a radio, you must dial down the external volume. Only then does the signal become audible.

Ask yourself:

- Am I attached to a specific outcome?
- Am I trying to sound smart, or be of service?
- Can I trust that *what needs to arise, will*?

Intuition is humble. It does not seek to impress, it seeks to connect.

## The Pitfall: When Intuition Isn't Intuition

Sometimes what we think is intuition is actually bias.

It might be:

- *Projection*: You see your own story in the client's.
- *Assumption*: You've heard similar words from other clients, so you jump to a pattern.
- *Emotionally charged*: You're reacting, not receiving.

True intuition feels calm, spacious, and non-urgent. Bias often feels tight, emotional, and convincing.

Here's a simple test:

*Does this insight feel grounded and generous, or does it feel urgent and personal?*

When in doubt, pause. Let it breathe. If it's intuition, it will return with clarity. If bias rears its head, it will dissolve in the light of stillness.

## The Coach's Responsibility

With great sensitivity comes great responsibility.

When sharing intuitive impressions:

- Use neutral language.
- Stay curious, not certain.
- Honor the client's agency, always.

Intuition is for *illuminating* the path. Your role is not to direct the client, but to walk beside them with a lantern.

## Case Study: Trusting the Inner Knowing

Client: Leila, 38, a marketing executive.
Presenting Goal: *"I want to improve my team leadership skills."*

In early sessions, she focused on delegation and time management. But something in her energy felt… detached. Mechanical.

In one session, as she spoke about her team, I felt an unusual pressure in my chest, a tightness that didn't belong to me. At the same time, an image came to mind: Leila in a boat, paddling alone while others sat passively, watching.

Instead of interpreting it, I said gently:

*"Leila, may I share something that just came up for me? I had an image of you rowing a boat alone, while others watched. I'm wondering: do you feel like you're carrying more than your share?"*

Her eyes filled with tears.

*"I feel like no one actually sees how hard I'm trying. I keep doing more, hoping they'll respect me. But I'm exhausted."*

From there, the real work began, not on delegation, but on worthiness, boundaries, and leadership rooted in self-trust.

## Intuition Awakens Intuition

When we coach with intuition, we awaken it in our clients. Trusting and using intuition, letting it guide, makes it sharper, and it begins to feel more comfortable.

As you model trust in your inner knowing, the client may begin to listen to their own. They discover that the answers are not "out there", they are within.

And that is the greatest gift we can offer.

Intuition is not a shortcut. It is not a party trick. It is a sacred art, a listening beyond listening and may not always make sense. It *will* be meaningful if we learn to respect its rhythms, its subtleties, its sacred silences.

Coaching with intuition is not about being right. It's about being *real.* It's about showing up with a heart that listens, a mind that observes, and a presence that trusts.

When you coach from that place, the conversation becomes more than coaching : it's a ripple of transformation.

**Reflective Questions**

1. *What are my signals that intuition is speaking; body, breath, images?*
2. *How can I distinguish between intuitive insight and bias?*
3. *When have I offered something intuitive that shifted the conversation?*
4. *What helps me become quiet enough to hear my intuition?*

# Chapter 9: Coaching the Whole Person with Alignment

***"The purpose of our journey is to restore ourselves to wholeness."*** *- Debbie Ford*

## The Journey from Fragmentation to Wholeness

Coaching grounded in spiritual intelligence sees the client not as a problem to solve, but as a whole being in evolution. This approach welcomes all aspects of the person—logic, emotion, energy, belief, identity, intuition. It recognizes that beneath every goal is a yearning, and beneath every resistance, a truth waiting to be honored.

Whole-person coaching does not compartmentalize the client into roles or labels. It engages with the layers beneath the surface. The stories they tell themselves, the values they live by, the fears they've inherited, the quiet longing they've never voiced. It is here that real transformation happens; not in fixing what is broken, but in remembering what is whole.

This approach requires a shift in the coach's mindset. It calls for presence that listens beyond words, for questions that emerge from deep stillness, and for an ability to honor the client's internal authority without imposing structure too quickly. It invites a reverence for mystery—a willingness to work with the invisible forces that shape a person's journey.

When coaching evolves in this way, it stops being a linear process and becomes a sacred dialogue. The client does not just discover new goals. They reconnect with their own inner compass. And from that place, the external shifts: career, relationships, leadership, decisions; become expressions of something much deeper: alignment with their truest self.

We often meet clients at the crossroads of change, torn between what they do, what they feel, and who they long to become. Their lives might look successful on paper, but something inside feels misaligned. That internal tug-of-war is more than stress or indecision; it is a call for alignment.

To coach the whole person is to honor the sacred intersection of thoughts, emotions, and spirit, the full spectrum of human experience. It is to listen not only to what is being said, but to the quiet signals beneath the surface: the emotional tension, the flicker in their voice when they mention something meaningful, the pause that signals longing. Coaching becomes an act of witnessing the inner orchestra and helping the client tune each instrument until harmony is restored.

## Integrating Mind, Emotions, and Spirit

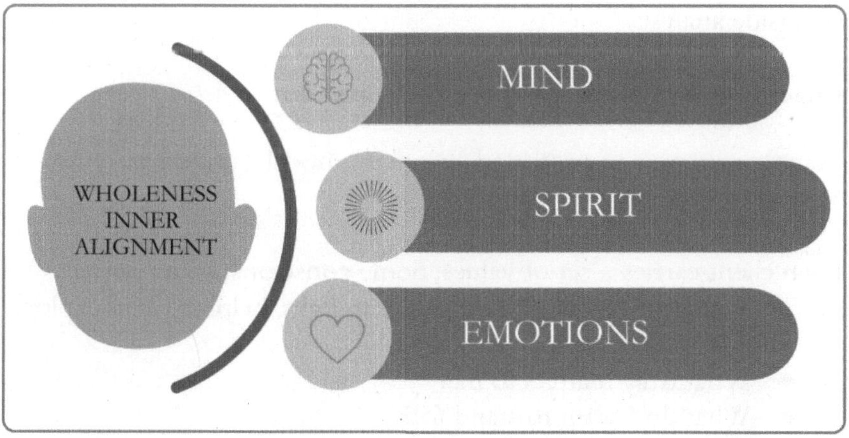


Alignment begins when we coach beyond behavior. At its core, it asks three essential questions:

- Mind: What does the client believe?
- Emotions: What do they feel and desire?
- Spirit: What do they yearn for at a soul level?

Clients often come with goals around productivity or performance, but deeper listening reveals unmet emotional needs or a spiritual hunger for meaning. For instance, a leader may want to improve team engagement but underneath lies a longing to be seen and valued, not just for results, but for who they are.

When we bring the whole self into coaching, change becomes more than behavioral. It becomes embodied. The client adopts a new habit; they begin to live a different story.

Each aspect, mind, heart, and spirit offer a unique intelligence. When disconnected, the client may live in performance mode: productive but unfulfilled, efficient but emotionally exhausted.

True coaching does not compartmentalize. It holds space for integration, where logic meets emotion, and intuition is honored alongside analysis.

**Coaching for Values, Purpose & Alignment**

There's a simple but profound alignment model I use often:
Values → Purpose → Action

Each client carries a set of values. Some conscious, some buried. Our role as coaches is to bring those values to light, helping them explore:

- What truly matters to me?
- What do I want to stand for?
- Where am I compromising, and why?

From there, we move into *purpose:* not as a grand mission statement, but as a felt sense of meaning. Purpose doesn't have to be big and bold.

Sometimes, it's a quiet whisper: *"I want to create a kinder workplace,"* or *"I want to parent with presence."*

And from purpose flows aligned action, choices that feel right not just logically, but emotionally and spiritually. This is where transformation sticks. The shift is not performative; it's embodied.

When actions begin to flow from purpose and are rooted in authentic values, alignment takes shape. Life feels less like a constant push and more like a river in flow. The inner tension eases. Integrity returns.

**At the center, where all three converge, is wholeness, 'The *Trinity of Alignment*'**

This is where the coaching magic happens. Where clarity becomes wisdom, where purpose meets action, and where clients begin to live with internal coherence.

As coaches, we often hear clients say, "*I know what I should do, but I just don't do it.*" Or "*I want this, but something keeps getting in the way.*" What they're often describing is misalignment, between values and actions, inner wisdom and outer obligations, logic and longing.

Supporting clients begins with deep listening, not just to the content of their goals but to the deeper energy beneath their words. Alignment becomes possible when:

- Clients are encouraged to articulate their true values, not borrowed from society or culture, but arising from lived experience and emotional truth
- They are supported in exploring their core purpose, not as an abstract concept but as an animating force already present in their lives
- They're invited to notice where their actions feel in harmony with their values and purpose, and where they don't

A powerful moment often occurs when a client realizes, "*No wonder I feel exhausted, I've been succeeding at someone else's dream.*"

This is when coaching transcends problem-solving and becomes soul-work.

A coach who models inner alignment becomes a mirror in which the client can see their own fragmentation; and their potential wholeness. This doesn't mean the coach has all the answers. It means the coach embodies presence, coherence, and humility. The coach doesn't just ask questions; they *listen with the whole being*, attuned to subtle dissonance between what the client says and what their body, tone, or energy may be revealing.

In this space, alignment becomes less about making something happen, and more about removing what's in the way: old stories, outdated roles, and emotional residues that no longer serve.

As a coach, tuning in to values, purpose and action allows you to notice where the client is leading from, and where there may be dissonance. Are they overthinking but emotionally numb? Spiritually curious but disconnected from action?

This trinity provides a compass for realignment.

## Integration with Buddhist and Hindu Philosophy

Ancient wisdom traditions have long explored the idea that transformation is not only personal, it is relational, contextual, and spiritual. A key Buddhist principle, *"When the mind changes, the environment changes"*, speaks to the deep interdependence between inner state and outer experience. This idea finds resonance in the Hindu notion of *yatha drishti, tatha srishti*, or, "*as your vision is, so is your world.*"

Both traditions invite a reframe: transformation is not about fixing the outside but about seeing from the inside out. Coaching, when practiced at depth, honors this orientation. We do not merely support clients in changing their behaviors; we support a shift in how they perceive reality, which then naturally alters how they act in it.

In the Bhagavad Gita, Lord Krishna speaks of *svabhava* (one's inherent nature) and *svadharma* (one's personal path or duty). Coaching alignment is about helping clients rediscover their *svabhava* and align their actions with *svadharma*, not as an imposed ideal but as an emerging inner truth.

In Buddhism, the concept of *Pratītyasamutpāda* or dependent origination tells us: nothing arises independently, our inner states and external reality co-arise and co-influence. As the Buddha taught, "*With this as condition, that arises.*" Thus, a shift in the inner world, thoughts, intentions, awareness' inevitably affects the outer world.

When a client starts to move in accordance with their inner truth, they find greater ease, clarity, and impact. Their relationships shift. Their teams respond differently. The world seems to reflect a new order, not because the world has changed, but because they have.

## Creating the Field for Wholeness

The coaching space becomes sacred not because of rituals or dogma, it is a field where *wholeness is remembered.* The coach holds the paradox: seeing the client as already whole while also journeying with them through fragmentation.

This requires a deep sense of presence, not performance. When a coach sits in that quality of awareness, they can sense when something is out of tune. It might show up as a pause, a shift in breathing, or a flicker in the client's eye. These are not distractions. These are the threads that lead us deeper into integration.

Wholeness emerges not from analysis alone, but from inner resonance. When mind, emotions, and spirit come into conversation with one another, the client begins to recognize their own symphony.

*A coach doesn't conduct this music, they help the client tune their own instrument.*

## Inner Dialogue: Coaching for Alignment

When a client feels stuck or split between two choices, consider asking:

- "What part of you is not yet on board?"
- "Which voice in you wants to move forward, and which one hesitates?"
- "Is your decision aligned with your values, or is it shaped by someone else's expectations?"

These questions open the door to alignment, by honoring the inner resistance and not forcing compliance. The resistance could be the emotions that haven't caught up yet, or the spiritual discomfort that signals deeper truth.

Additionally, this 3-step process and inquiry can help clients align from the inside out:

**Step 1: Pause.**

Slow down the pace. Ask the client to notice their breath, their body, their inner state.

**Step 2: Listen Within.**

Invite them to notice:

- What is your head saying?
- What is your heart saying?
- What is your soul nudging you toward?

**Step 3: Realign & Ask**

- "If you honored all three voices: mind, heart, and spirit, what would you choose?"
- "What action feels most congruent with your whole self?"

This tool is especially powerful when a client is grappling with difficult choices, burnout, or a sense of disconnection.

## Lasting Transformation Requires Wholeness

Change that excludes the self is temporary. You can change jobs, cities, or habits—but if the internal fracture remains, discontent will resurface in a different form. Lasting transformation occurs when clients feel seen in their entirety: as thinkers or doers, as feeling, sensing, evolving beings.

This is where neuroscience meets wisdom. The brain thrives on coherence: when beliefs, emotions, and actions match, it reduces internal stress. Similarly, the spirit awakens when life begins to feel true to one's essence. Emotional integration helps regulate the nervous system, while spiritual insight fuels resilience.

Coaching the whole person is restoring inner congruence.

## Case Study: The Journey to Wholeness

Client Name: Nina, Marketing head in a global firm

When I first met Nina, she was known for her sharp strategy and relentless drive. On paper, she had it all. She began the session with a single statement:

*"I feel like I'm living someone else's life."*

As we unpacked her story, patterns emerged. Her success was built on values passed down by her family: security, status, recognition. But internally, Nina yearned for creativity, contribution, and community. Her spirit was starving, even as her mind was excelling.

Through our sessions, we explored this fragmentation: with compassionate curiosity without judgment. She began to name her real values: freedom, joy, connection. We aligned these with a renewed sense of purpose: to build storytelling campaigns that inspired social impact.

What followed wasn't a dramatic career change, but a soulful pivot. She stayed in marketing, but chose projects that aligned with her values. She brought more of her authentic self into meetings. And most importantly, she stopped living on autopilot.

The lasting shift? She began living in integrity, as a lived experience.

## Holding the Mirror of Wholeness

As coaches, our presence becomes a mirror. When we show up as whole, mindfully aware, emotionally grounded, and spiritually attuned, we effectively invite the client into that same state of inner coherence. It's imperative to evoke awareness to support alignment in areas like:

- What are they masking?
- Where do they feel the emotion in their body?
- If their inner wisdom had a voice right now, what would it say?
- Where are their values and actions out of sync?
- What would it look like to bring their whole self into this situation?

And sometimes, the most powerful prompt is silence. It's the sacred pause that lets the client hear themselves more deeply.

We must learn to transition into the state of 'Conscious Competence' to evolve to 'Unconscious Competence' to notice the minor misalignments; a fleeting expression, a shift in posture, a dissonant phrase like *"I guess I have to…"* These are clues that something deeper needs attention.

Alignment is rarely dramatic. It is often found in gentle nudges, course corrections, and the return to stillness. When you learn to hold space for the small moments, the deeper shifts follow.

## Coaching Implication: Wholeness is Alignment Across All Realms

We often begin by observing the external reality of our clients. Their goals, challenges, environments. But real change happens when we help them see how their inner world shapes the outer one.

When a coach integrates these philosophies into practice, the coaching space transitions from being just a conversation to an evolved & sacred ground for alignment. For a coach working in this realm, the client is a dynamic field of thoughts, emotions, spirit, and karmic memory; and not a goal-seeking individual. A shift in self-awareness alters not only how we act, but also how the world responds. As we grow in emotional intelligence and spiritual clarity, we influence our surroundings in subtle yet powerful ways.

Clients who cultivate peace within begin to experience less conflict around them. Leaders who align with their purpose find their teams more motivated. Parents who heal old wounds raise more resilient children.

Thus, coaching the whole person is not just about individual evolution. It is a ripple, one that touches relationships, organizations, and communities. When the self transforms, the world mirrors back that change.

## Reflection: The Inner Pilgrimage

To coach with alignment is to *believe* that clients are not broken, they *are* whole and complete, capable of focusing inwards to find & create their own solutions. Our role is not to fix or advise, but to create space for remembering, the gathering of the scattered self into an integrated whole.

In the quiet unfolding of their truth, the client becomes their own compass. And from that centered place, transformation doesn't feel like effort, it feels like homecoming. In alignment, the client begins to access clarity, and a quiet, inner knowing. And when we coach from that space of trust and attunement, we enter the realm of intuition; the invisible guide within.

Let us now step into that space…

Invite your clients into this process. Give them space to explore *what* they want, and *why* , along with what truly fits *who* they are becoming. This simple audit often opens doors to deeper truths. The *how* will come forth, through the intrinsic motivation and commitment they will discover on this inward journey.

# Chapter 10: The Tangible Measure of the Intangible

## *Spiritual Brain: Transcendence, Purpose, and the Neural Pathways Within*

What if the longing for purpose, the quiet pull toward something larger than ourselves, was a philosophical yearning based on a neurological impulse?

In recent years, neuroscience has begun to illuminate what mystics and spiritual traditions have long intuited: the human brain is wired for transcendence. Purpose and meaning are not merely abstract ideas but are intimately linked to specific brain regions and processes that shape our decisions, regulate our emotions, and guide our moral compass.

Central to this understanding is the Default Mode Network (DMN): a constellation of interconnected brain regions that activates when we are not focused on the outside world. This network lights up during introspection, self-referential thought, imagination, and reflection, precisely the mental space we enter when contemplating our purpose or engaging in spiritual practices. When coaches hold a space for clients to explore "Who am I?" or "What matters most to me?", they are quite literally inviting them to activate and reorganize this powerful inner network.

Interestingly, during deep meditation or spiritual states, the activity in the DMN tends to quiet down. This temporary deactivation correlates with a sense of ego-dissolution, interconnectedness, and timeless awareness; states that many clients describe when they experience breakthrough moments in coaching. These transcendent experiences aren't abstract. They correspond to measurable shifts in the brain;

moments when the boundaries of the self-soften, and something more expansive emerges.

Neuroscience also reveals the role of the prefrontal cortex, which governs ethical decision-making, foresight, and empathy: capacities essential for purpose-driven leadership. When clients engage in meaningful reflection and values clarification, these areas show increased activation. Over time, practices like journaling, coaching dialogue, and intentional silence can strengthen neural pathways that support compassion, intentionality, and clarity of direction.

Purpose, then, is not just an idea, it is a neurobiological orientation. When we coach clients toward purpose, we are engaging their very biology in the service of transformation. We're not just asking powerful questions; we are reshaping patterns of brain activity, gently guiding the client from the noise of external demands toward the inner music of meaning.

In coaching the invisible, we work with this profound architecture: softly, skillfully, reverently. For it is here, in the silent conversation between neurons and soul, that the deepest shifts begin.

## From Brainwaves to Breakthroughs: The Role of Brain States in Deep Coaching

Beneath the surface of every coaching conversation, a silent symphony is playing; electrical rhythms pulsing through the brain, shaping the client's receptivity, insight, and integration. Understanding these brainwave states offers coaches a powerful lens through which to facilitate deeper, more transformational work.

The human brain operates across a spectrum of electrical frequencies, each associated with distinct states of consciousness:

- Beta waves (13–30 Hz): Dominant during focused, analytical thought. Most coaching sessions begin here, clients arriving with challenges, ideas, or problems to solve.

- Alpha waves (8–12 Hz): Linked to relaxation and receptivity. Coaches help clients transition into this state through calm presence, mindful pauses, and reflective inquiry.
- Theta waves (4–8 Hz): Associated with insight, memory, and deep creativity. This is often the realm of breakthroughs; when a well-placed question lands in silence and something shifts.
- Delta waves (0.5–4 Hz): Present in deep, dreamless sleep, but also momentarily accessed during states of profound inner stillness.
- Gamma waves (30–100 Hz): Found in moments of heightened perception, compassion, and spiritual unity, especially during deep meditation or transcendent experiences.

When a coach cultivates spaciousness, emotional safety, and resonance, they invite the client into slower brainwave frequencies where the busy mind quiets and the deeper self begins to speak. These altered states are not mystical accidents; they are neurological doorways into clarity and transformation.

This awareness also reframes silence in coaching. A long pause is not just a technique, it may be the client's brain dropping into theta, where disparate ideas reorganize into insight. Similarly, breathwork, guided visualizations, or somatic check-ins can help shift brain states deliberately, enhancing neuroplasticity and integration.

Seasoned coaches often sense this shift intuitively. A client becomes softer, slower, more inward. Their language shifts from the head to the heart. In those moments, the coach is not merely listening, they are holding the brain in a new rhythm, creating space for inner wisdom to emerge.

When we understand brainwaves, we begin to see that coaching is not only a cognitive process; it is an energetic and neurological one. Coaches become facilitators of altered states that reconnect clients with their deepest knowing. In doing so, we honor the invisible as a living field; within the brain, the body, and beyond.

## The Gut–Brain Axis: Coaching from the Core of Inner Knowing

We often say, "Trust your gut"; but what if that wisdom is more than metaphor?

Modern neuroscience has validated what ancient traditions have always known: the gut is a second brain, rich with neurons, neurochemicals, and intuitive intelligence. The gut–brain axis is a bidirectional communication system linking the gastrointestinal system and the central nervous system, influencing everything from mood to decision-making.

This visceral intelligence, also known as interoception, allows us to perceive internal bodily signals; like tightness in the chest, butterflies in the stomach, or a sudden sense of calm. These signals often arrive before cognitive awareness, offering clues to what is aligned, what is off, and what is calling to be noticed.

In coaching, this becomes a sacred resource.

When a client says, "I just know this isn't right," or "I can't explain it, but I feel drawn to this path," they are speaking from this embodied intelligence. It's not irrational; it's pre-rational, often more accurate than logic because it reflects the whole-body sensing system rather than isolated mental analysis.

As coaches, we can help clients tune into this intelligence by:

- Slowing down the conversation and inviting a somatic check-in: *"What does your body say when you imagine choosing this?"*
- Exploring felt sensations as data: *"You said your chest feels heavy-what might that be telling you?"*
- Validating non-verbal knowing: *"You seem to know something, even if the words aren't there yet. Would you like to stay with that for a moment?"*

These micro-interventions allow clients to shift attention from thought to sensation, from intellect to inner alignment. Over time, they learn to access the body as a compass, one that is often more attuned to truth than the conditioned mind.

For the coach, cultivating your own interoceptive awareness is equally essential. When you sense tightness, warmth, or unease in your own body during a session, it might signal resonance or dissonance with the client's process. Used skillfully, your own somatic awareness becomes a coaching instrument, guiding presence and intuition in the moment.

In *Coaching the Invisible*, this is where form meets flow, where spiritual intelligence is grounded in biology. Coaching doesn't only happen in the mind; it emerges from the whole self. And when the body is welcomed into the conversation, transformation becomes not only visible, but deeply felt.

## Neuroplasticity and the Sacred: How Spiritual Practices Rewire the Brain

The most profound shifts in coaching often occur not in the session itself, but in what the client practices between sessions. This is where spiritual intelligence meets neuroscience - when daily rituals, when practiced with intention, begin to rewire the brain.

At the heart of this transformation is neuroplasticity—the brain's lifelong ability to reorganize itself by forming new neural connections. Neuroscience has shown that consistent practices such as meditation, gratitude, and compassion physically alter brain structures. Regions associated with empathy, regulation, and perspective-taking grow denser. Meanwhile, the stress centers of the brain, like the amygdala, shrink in size and reactivity.

Consider meditation. Studies have found that even eight weeks of mindfulness practice can increase gray matter density in the hippocampus (associated with learning and memory) and in structures related to self-awareness and compassion. At the same time, it reduces activity in the default mode network, calming the self-referential mind that often traps clients in looping thought patterns.

Gratitude is no less powerful. When clients engage in regular gratitude journaling, they begin to strengthen neural pathways associated with optimism and emotional resilience. The act of noticing the good reshapes the lens through which they see the world; not by denial of struggle, but by rebalancing the narrative toward wholeness.

Compassion-based practices, such as loving-kindness meditation, not only expand emotional capacity but have been linked to increased activity in the insula and prefrontal cortex—regions tied to empathy and ethical decision-making. These are foundational traits in spiritually intelligent leadership and relational coaching.

When coaches integrate these practices into their work—not as prescriptions, but as invitations—they support clients in more than self-awareness. They facilitate structural transformation in the brain. Over time, clients become not just more aware, but more capable of sustaining calm, accessing intuition, and leading from alignment.

In this light, coaching becomes not just a journey of insight, but of re-patterning—the invisible made real through repetition and reverence. The sacred is not separate from science. In fact, it's embedded in the way neurons fire, habits form, and consciousness expands.

When a coach helps a client commit to even one small daily practice—ten minutes of stillness, one act of compassion, a moment of presence—they are initiating not only a shift in behavior, but a profound shift in brain and being.

## Transcendence in Leadership: Coaching Beyond Self into Sacred Impact

At the highest levels of human development, leadership becomes less about power and more about presence. Less about influence and more about integration—of values, of self, and of something greater. This is where spiritual intelligence enters not just as a concept, but as a leadership imperative.

Transcendence, in coaching, is not the escape from the self. It is the expansion of identity beyond the ego, beyond roles and outcomes, into a felt sense of connectedness—to purpose, to others, to the planet, or to the divine, however the client defines it.

What neuroscience now confirms is that this expanded state is not merely a mystical experience; it is a biologically accessible state. Moments of awe, purpose, and moral elevation activate regions of the brain associated with prosocial behavior, visionary thinking, and long-term decision-making. This is precisely what distinguishes great leaders from good ones.

When we coach for transcendence, we support clients in:

- Shifting from ambition to contribution: Moving the locus of leadership from personal achievement to legacy and impact.
- Developing vertical awareness: Helping clients witness their inner landscape from a higher vantage point—not just *what* they think, but *how* they are thinking and *who* they are becoming.
- Aligning power with humility: Cultivating leaders who lead from centeredness rather than control, from clarity rather than fear.

This is not about idealism. In fact, it is one of the most practical outcomes of deep coaching. Leaders who operate from purpose and transcendence have been shown to foster more resilient cultures, make values-aligned decisions, and sustain performance under uncertainty.

Spiritual intelligence becomes their internal compass in complexity.

And for the coach, the role is to midwife this emergence; to hold space for the invisible architecture of leadership to take shape. This means attuning to the spiritual dimension of the client's experience without imposing belief systems. It means recognizing that breakthrough often comes not from strategy, but from surrender. And it means honoring the possibility that, in every coaching conversation, something larger is trying to unfold.

When clients touch transcendence, even briefly, something reorients within. They no longer lead from the surface, but from source. And in that shift, coaching becomes more than performance support—it becomes a spiritual act of service.

Would you like me to now group all five of these suggestions into a proposed Part III of the book? Or are you planning to publish these as a separate extended edition or companion guide?

## Tracking the Invisible: How We Measure What We Cannot See

In the realm of intangible coaching; where we work with energy, awareness, emotions, and spiritual insight, the question inevitably arises: *How do we track progress when transformation is largely invisible?* Unlike traditional metrics that rely on tangible KPIs or behavioral outputs, the invisible shifts we cultivate often show up subtly, gradually, and deeply. This is where coaching the invisible becomes both an art and a responsibility.

### 1. An Emotional-Spiritual Progress Tracker

To bridge the seen and unseen, I often invite clients into a co-created tracking process that blends emotional intelligence (EQ) and spiritual intelligence (SQ). One simple tool is a Quadrant Tracker, where clients assess themselves weekly or monthly across four axes:

| Quadrant | Focus Area | Sample Reflection Question |
|---|---|---|
| EQ-Internal | Emotional Self-Awareness & Regulation | How did I respond to emotional triggers this week? |
| EQ-External | Empathy & Relational Awareness | How connected and compassionate did I feel with others? |
| SQ-Internal | Alignment with Inner Values | Did I live in integrity with what matters most? |
| SQ-External | Purposeful Action & Contribution | Did I act from service, or react from ego? |

Over time, clients begin to *see the invisible*—not in what they do, but in *how* they show up. This is not a test. It's a mirror.

## 2. Journaling Prompts and Pattern Reflection

Another powerful practice I recommend is themed journaling across the coaching journey. Prompts such as:

- "What emotion did I listen to and honor today?"
- "Where did I override my intuition—and what was the cost?"
- "What am I becoming more of?"

These simple lines become tracking threads. Clients often discover themes: emotional triggers softening, values becoming non-negotiable, or synchronicities aligning with their intentions. As a coach, I watch these patterns emerge like constellations across our sessions, each reflection a star.

## 3. The Intangible Wheel of Life

Adapt the classic *Wheel of Life* to measure internal states rather than external domains. For example:

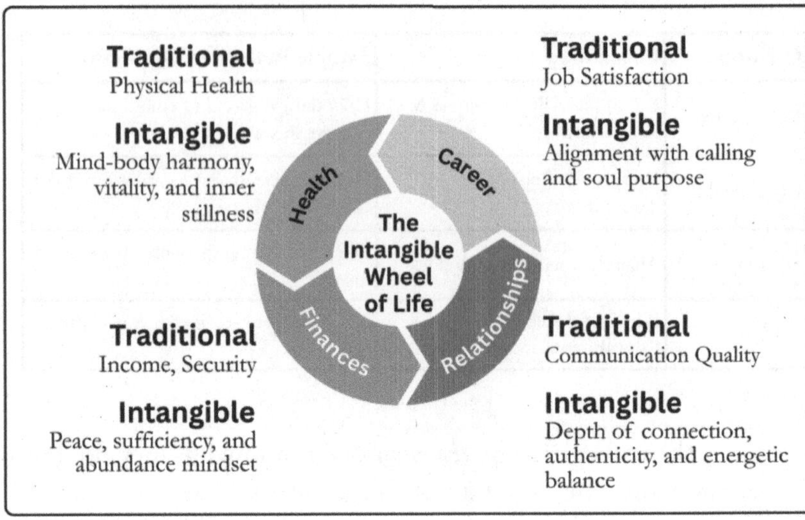


This tool helps clients visualize growth in domains that don't show up in a spreadsheet but govern the *quality* of their entire life experience.

**4. Stories from the Field: Coaching the Invisible Shift**

Over the years, I've witnessed clients who, on the surface, seemed to make no dramatic change. But then came the quiet transformation:

- A senior executive who used to avoid conflict begins asking clarifying questions in boardrooms; not from anger, but presence.
- A life coach burdened by comparison begins honoring her unique voice, and her client list doubles, without a single marketing push.
- A client grieving an old identity suddenly notices how much calmer they feel, how mornings are no longer rushed but sacred.

In each case, the evidence of transformation arrived not in action, but in energy.

## 5. Metrics That Matter: A New Tale of Transformation

In the realm of deep coaching, not all change can' or should be measured in hard metrics. Some of the most profound shifts occur beneath the surface, catalyzing visible transformation only after a foundational realignment has taken place. These are not soft indicators. They are *transformational anchors*; inner recalibrations that often serve as the root cause of long-term performance shifts. When we trace the journey of transformation, it becomes evident that outward success is frequently preceded by invisible, internal shifts.

For instance, a fear of conflict, when explored and released, gives rise to the courage to speak up. This seemingly subtle change in internal landscape often results in a marked increase in leadership presence and clarity. Similarly, self-doubt, when transformed into trust in one's intuition, leads to quicker, values-aligned decision-making—decisions that feel right not just logically, but viscerally. Overthinking, a hallmark of mental noise, gives way to embodied awareness. As this shift deepens, stress diminishes, and team dynamics become more harmonious and attuned.

Another common yet often overlooked pattern is a lack of purpose. When clients reconnect with meaning and anchor themselves in something deeper than day-to-day goals, they tap into a wellspring of intrinsic motivation and consistent engagement. And for those fixated on results, learning to surrender to the process does not weaken performance; it strengthens resilience. With this surrender comes a profound peace with whatever outcomes arise, allowing them to navigate uncertainty with grace and strength.

By learning to name and track these inner-to-outer pathways, we open new doors for measurement in coaching; ones that reflect the depth, sustainability, and soul of transformation, the *silent architecture* of meaningful change. They are *transformational anchors;* and often, the root cause of performance shifts.

### 6. Pre/Post Reflection Tools

To make the intangible tangible, introduce structured reflection at the beginning and end of every coaching engagement. Examples include:

Opening Questions:

- What emotions currently dominate your inner world?
- What do you long to become more of?
- Where do you feel out of sync with your values?

Closing Questions (3 or 6 months later):

- What has softened in you?
- Where do you respond instead of react?
- How does your inner landscape feel different now?

These become powerful bookends, showing clients what they may not have noticed had you not invited their awareness to it.

### 7. The Coach's Inner Instrument: Tracking Resonance and Shift

Perhaps the most refined tool is the coach's own awareness. As we develop mastery, we begin to track transformation not only in client words, but in tone, rhythm, metaphor, silence, and energy. Subtle changes like:

- The client pauses more often—there is now space between thought and speech.
- Their metaphors shift—from "being stuck in a swamp" to "walking through an open field."
- Their voice carries more wholeness, less edge. More certainty, less grasping.

This is where the coach *as an instrument* becomes sacred. We tune into frequency as much as fact. We witness shifts not as outcomes, but as emergence.

## Final Thought: What Gets Noticed, Grows

By weaving these tools and stories into your coaching container, you help clients notice what they might have otherwise missed. And in doing so, you validate their growth through action, and through being.

The invisible, once named, becomes sacred ground for transformation.

# Part Four

# The Coaching Playbook: Turning Insights into Action

After walking the winding path through the heart of coaching, exploring the mind, navigating emotions, and awakening the spirit, we arrive at the confluence where insight meets implementation.

The earlier parts of this book invited you into the depth of being: how to see the client beneath the story, feel their emotional truth, and listen to the whispers of their inner wisdom. Now, let's turn our gaze forward - with the same depth of presence, to the "how" of coaching.

This part is not a toolbox in the traditional sense. It is a synthesis of everything we've uncovered: the neuroscience that underpins behavior change, the emotional intelligence that sustains transformation, and the spiritual intelligence that lends it direction and purpose. Here, we explore how coaches can translate invisible shifts into visible outcomes, without losing the soul of the work.

You'll find frameworks, practices, and reflective exercises not as rigid structures, but as *living maps*, guides that adapt and respond to each client's unique terrain. These are not prescriptive formulas but invitations to co-create change, staying rooted in presence while remaining agile in process.

We also look ahead.

The final chapter of this part speaks to the evolving horizon of coaching. As the world turns, faster and more complex, so too must our role as coaches. What does it mean to coach in the age of AI? How do we keep the human heart at the center of our practice, even as technology advances? And how do we, as coaches, continue our own journey of mastery, learning not just new techniques, but new ways of *being*?

This section is for the coach who knows that transformation is both inner and outer, subtle and strategic. That insight, though powerful, must be anchored in deliberate action. And that our greatest tool is our mindful, evolving, present self-woven into the structure and methodology.

Let us now bring all the inner shifts to life, one intentional conversation at a time.

# Chapter 11: Designing Coaching Interventions That Stick

***"Integration is a basic law of life; when we resist it, disintegration is the natural result, both inside and outside of us. Thus we come to the concept of harmony through integration."*** - *Norman Cousins*

## The Sacred Architecture of Transformation

Coaching is an intentional, sacred conversation with the soul supported body of techniques. In this space, we *facilitate remembering*, a return to inner knowing, buried beneath layers of defense, disconnection, and self-doubt. Each session lays down stones of safety, awareness, and meaning. For these stones to become a lasting structure, we must engage the client's nervous system, emotional core, and spiritual compass. Each coaching session is therefore a brick in the architecture of transformation, a structure that must be strong enough to weather resistance, and fluid enough to allow for emergence.

Each of these pillars supports a distinct layer of human experience: *the biological, the emotional, and the existential.* When we design coaching interventions that speak to all three, we create sustainable, embodied transformation. When we ignore anyone, change remains surface-level, momentarily inspiring but ultimately unstable.

As we coach beneath the surface, navigating beliefs, values, identity, and soul, we are also weaving together the invisible threads of how human beings grow and transform. Change does not happen through insight alone. It becomes sustainable when the mind feels safe, the heart feels heard, and the soul feels seen.

This is where the '*Triv* becomes a *geni of Transformation*' guiding compass.

*In Vedic tradition, the Triveni Sangam, the confluence of the* ***Ganga, Yamuna,*** *and the invisible* ***Saraswati,*** *is a site of immense spiritual power. In coaching, too, transformation flows from the meeting point of three sacred rivers within the client: the biological intelligence of the brain, the emotional truth of the heart, and the guiding wisdom of the soul. This is the* ***'Triveni of Transformation'****, a model that reminds us that no sustainable change is purely cognitive, emotional, or spiritual. It is the integration of all three that builds lasting inner architecture.*

This architecture of transformation cannot stand on a single pillar. For insight to transform into integration, the coaching process must engage the client's neuroscience (the brain), emotional intelligence (the heart), and spiritual intelligence (the soul). This is how these 3 pillars play out in coaching:

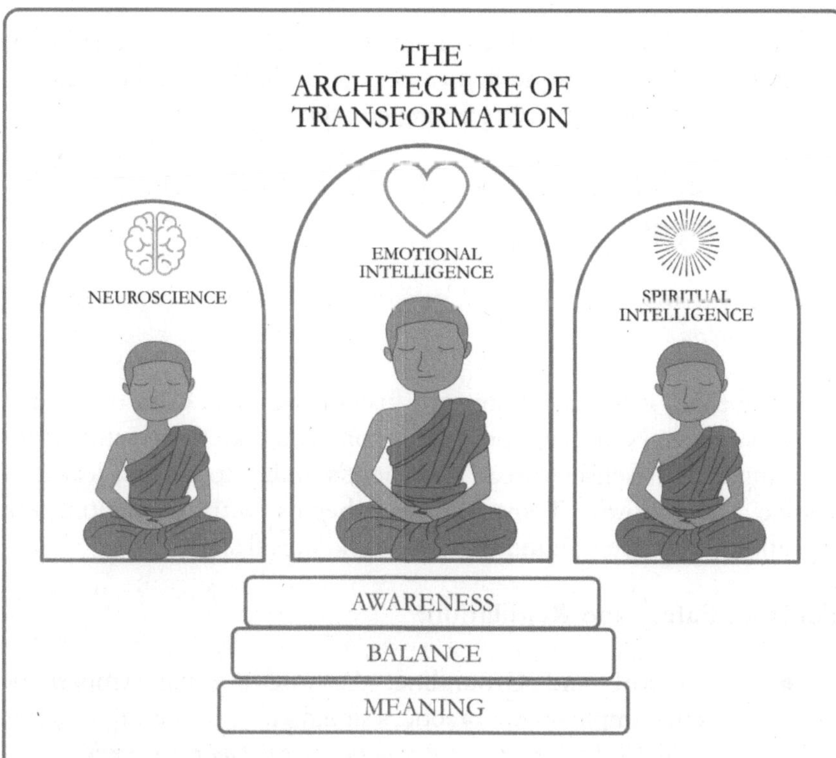


*The Triveni of Transformation: Coaching with Three Intelligences*

| Intelligence | What It Represents | Coaching Focus & Tools |
|---|---|---|
| Neuroscience | The brain's biology: safety, regulation, integration | Nervous system mapping, breathwork, grounding rituals |
| Emotional Intelligence | The heart's truth: emotional insight and integration | Somatic mapping, naming emotions, parts dialogue, emotional rehearsal |
| Spiritual Intelligence | The soul's compass: purpose, meaning, sacred identity | Sacred Why inquiry, future self, archetypes, symbolic rituals |

When the brain, heart, and soul align, coaching becomes sacred architecture.

Let's now explore each of these intelligences that cannot be effective as separate silos. The magic & miracles are evident when these sacred streams flow through every coaching conversation.

## Pillar One: The Brain Needs Safety to Learn (Neuroscience)

*When the nervous system is hijacked, no insight can land. It's like trying to plant seeds in a storm.*

Before we can guide clients toward insight, we must calm the body's primal systems. Neuroception, our unconscious safety detector: scans for danger. If it senses threat, the client's ability to reflect, learn, or change shuts down. Transformation begins with regulation, not cognition. Presence is a mindset; a physiological state.

**Tools for Safety and Regulation:**

- Breathwork and Grounding: Activate the parasympathetic system. Simple breath practices signal safety to the vagus nerve. Ask: *"What happens if we pause to feel your feet on the ground?"*
- Polyvagal-informed Coaching: Recognize states of fight, flight, or freeze. Be curious: *"What's your body telling you right now?"*

- Rituals for Safety: Lighting a candle, choosing a calming object, anchoring with breath. These invite predictability and familiarity, which the nervous system craves.

These practices shift the client from survival to receptivity, where learning and transformation begin.

Creating safety is not a one-time intervention; it is a continuous invitation. Coaches who master this first pillar find that even the most complex insights land with surprising ease, because the body is finally ready to receive.

## Pillar Two: Emotions are the Gatekeepers of Insight (Emotional Intelligence)

*Emotion is energy in motion. If it's stuck, so are we.*

Once the body is settled, emotions begin to speak. Our job is not to fix but to witness, name, and integrate emotional data. Emotions hold truth, about what matters, what's unresolved, what longs to be healed.

Along with coaching tangible goals, we are coaching the *emotional climate* in which those goals either flourish or falter. Unexpressed fear, guilt, shame, grief, or anger can sabotage the best intentions. When we partner with emotion as a source of intelligence, we become guides for healing as well as growth.

**Tools for Emotional Integration:**

- Name It to Tame It: Invite clients to label core emotions. Language creates containment. *"If this emotion had a name, what would it be?"*
- Somatic Mapping: Where in the body is this feeling? Emotions are somatic events. Mapping them builds body-emotion fluency. *"What shape does this feeling have? What texture?"*

- Parts Work: Let the inner critic speak. Let the protector explain. Let the child be heard. This creates internal dialogue, dismantling shame and allowing compassion.

The coach becomes a mirror and a container. We help clients meet themselves with grace.

But there is more. *Emotion is not just something to process, it is also the gateway to motivation.* Joy, passion, curiosity, love, these are what drive action. A coaching intervention is only sustainable when it engages the client's emotional fuel.

Expanding the Practice:

We can go even deeper by inviting emotional rehearsal. After identifying a desired shift, ask: *"How would that feel in your body if it were already true?"* Help the client *feel into the future* emotionally before they arrive there behaviorally. This leverages the brain's plasticity and emotional learning loops.

You can also support clients in emotionally releasing old patterns. Use creative processes like symbolic letter-writing, voice dialogues, or even somatic shaking. These practices, when used skillfully, clear space for new truths to land.

Reflection Pause:

- Do I attend to both pain and possibility in the emotional realm?
- What emotional responses in clients challenge *my own* regulation?
- Where might I be overusing cognition when emotion is calling for attention?

The second pillar invites *courage & resilience.* It asks the coach to sit with discomfort, to hold silence after tears, to not rush in with clarity when the client is still discovering their truth. In this space where emotion is allowed to breathe, transformation becomes inevitable.

## Pillar Three: Meaning is the Glue That Sticks (Spiritual Intelligence)

*The moment insight meets soul, it becomes wisdom.*

Insight without purpose fades. Real change sticks when it aligns with who the client is becoming in terms of their values, calling, and sacred "*why*." Spiritual Intelligence (SQ) invites us to coach beyond the surface toward the soul's architecture.

This pillar is often neglected because it feels intangible and therefore has no perceived value. It's also about the coach's own journey into this realm. "*A coach can take their client only as deep as they have been themselves*" (Rich Litvin) This is not about similar journeys or experiences; it's the awareness about the existence of the inward journey.

Yet it is precisely this intangibility that gives it power. Meaning anchors behavior in identity. It transforms "*I should*" into "*I must*" or even "*I am.*"

**Tools for Meaning-Making:**

- Future Self Dialogue: "If your wisest future self were here, what would they say?" This reframes decisions through the lens of legacy and evolution.
- Sacred Why Inquiry: "What's this really about?" "What are you willing to honor now?" These questions bring clients face to face with purpose.
- Spiritual Archetypes: Invite clients to explore inner archetypes (the Teacher, the Warrior, the Sage). These evoke deep inner guidance systems.

These tools change coaching from transactional to transformational.

Spiritual Intelligence also opens the door to mystery. It makes space for synchronicity, intuition, and the symbolic. Let's not shy away from a client's dreams, metaphors, or spiritual practices. They are often offering clues that logic cannot decipher.

Expanding the Practice:

Invite ritual as a tool for meaning. Ask clients to *create a symbolic act* to honor a decision, a walk, a letter to an ancestor, a mantra, or a small ceremony. These moments help crystallize transformation.

You can also explore liminal space with clients. These are the *"in-between"* moments, between resignation and clarity, between roles, between identities. Clients often experience confusion here. Instead of fixing it, help them stay with it. Ask: *"What is this space inviting you to become?"*

Meaning is rarely delivered, it is discovered. As coaches, our role is not to provide answers but to ask *better* questions, ones that reveal the sacred beneath the surface.

Reflection Pause:

- How do I define "spiritual" in my coaching?
- Do I allow space for silence, intuition, or mystery in my sessions?
- What happens when I treat each client's story as sacred?

## From Insight to Integration: Making it Stick

Insight is not enough. It must be ritualized, anchored, and revisited.

Integration requires repetition, reflection, and embodiment. It is not linear, it spirals. Clients revisit the same themes from different levels of awareness. Coaches who understand this don't rush the process, they *hold the container* long enough for true rewiring to occur.

Integration Practices:

- Designing Rituals: What will mark this shift? Even small gestures like a poem, a cup of tea, a shared breath, can become anchors.
- Neural Anchoring: Ask, "What will remind you of this shift every day?" It could be a bracelet, a wallpaper, or a post-it with a soul message.
- Reflective Journaling: Offer prompts to revisit emotional shifts and spiritual insights. Suggest: *"What has changed in how you see yourself?"*

Change doesn't necessarily happen in the coaching session. It happens in the quiet moments between them. Help your clients honor those moments.

## The Identity Iceberg: Coaching at Depth

Imagine a massive iceberg. At the tip: behaviors. Beneath: thoughts, feelings, beliefs, values, self-image, and core identity.

Your interventions must go below the waterline. We don't coach problems. We coach the inner architecture from which problems emerge.

But what does that really mean? Let's go deeper.

## The Identity Iceberg Model: Coaching the Whole Self

| Iceberg Layer | What to Explore | Coaching Entry Point |
|---|---|---|
| Behavior | Habits, actions, external performance | Goal setting, behavioral contracts |
| Skills/Strategies | Tools, competencies, task execution | Feedback, learning plans, resourcing |
| Beliefs | Narratives, mental models, assumptions | Reframing, cognitive challenge |
| Values | What matters, internal conflict, priorities | Values discovery, alignment coaching |
| Identity | Self-concept, roles, worthiness | Identity statements, parts work, mirror dialogue |
| Soul / Purpose | Calling, meaning, spiritual congruence | Sacred Why, archetypes, future self work |

The deeper the coaching, the more lasting the transformation.

Each level requires a different kind of listening. Surface-level change is efficient. Depth work is sacred. Both have their place and together they lead to lasting integration.

## Why Surface Change Doesn't Stick

Many clients appear to shift during coaching, only to revert months later. Often, it's not because the coaching wasn't good, it's because it didn't reach far enough. When interventions target behavior without touching identity, there's friction. The body remembers one thing, while the soul longs for another.

The deeper the shift, the more natural the change. When a client sees themselves differently, they *act* differently not because they must, but because they can't-*not.*

Coaching Questions That Dive Deeper

- What does this goal say about who you believe you are?
- Who are you when no one is watching?

- What identity are you trying to protect, or escape?
- What part of your soul is asking to emerge through this change?

These questions are not diagnostic; they are doorways. They invite the client to descend, gently, into the depth where the real shift is waiting.

*A Sacred Reminder*

The work below the waterline is not about fixing, it's about *remembering*. You're not creating change; you're revealing truth. The Iceberg is not a danger to avoid—it's the sacred terrain of the coaching journey.

## Case Study: A Framework in Action

The Client: Riya, a Senior Leader

Riya came with a presenting problem: "I need to be more assertive."

But beneath that:

- Her nervous system flared in conflict, rooted in early trauma.
- Her emotions spoke of shame and fear of rejection.
- Her spiritual self longed for inner congruence and purpose.

The Coaching Arc:

- Session 1: Breathwork and grounding. Nervous system mapping.
- Session 2-3: Naming emotions, parts dialogue, and self-compassion rituals.
- Session 4-6: Sacred Why coaching, future-self letter, creating a courage talisman.
- Session 7: Ritual closure and integration practice (symbolic river walk).

The Outcome:
Riya didn't just speak up in meetings, she rediscovered her inner

voice. Assertiveness was no longer a skill. It became a natural expression of a re-aligned identity.

*What began as performance coaching became a pilgrimage back to herself.*

## Mapping to ICF Core Competencies

| Coaching Tool / Principle | ICF Core Competency | Why It Matters |
|---|---|---|
| Nervous System Regulation | 4. Trust & Safety, 5. Presence | Calms fight/flight so learning can happen |
| Emotion Labeling (EQ) | 6. Listens Actively, 4.Trust & Safety | Emotional insight deepens self-awareness |
| Sacred Why Dialogue (SQ) | 3. Agreements, 7. Awareness | Aligns coaching to soul-level goals |
| Ritual Design & Anchoring | 8. Facilitates Growth | Supports lasting behavior change |
| Identity Iceberg Work | 7. Awareness, 6. Listening | Coaches inner patterns, not symptoms |

### Reflection Prompts for Coaches

- Where do I stop, at insight or at transformation?
- How do I regulate my own nervous system during sessions?
- What rituals do I offer my clients for integration?
- Which layer of the Iceberg do I tend to coach most?
- How can I better design interventions that engage all three intelligences — brain, heart, and soul?
- What would shift in my coaching if I treated every session as sacred architecture?
- How do I navigate ambiguity and trust emergence as part of the coaching process?

*Sticky coaching isn't about giving more tools. It's about going deeper: beneath behavior, beneath belief, into the soil where identity grows.*

## Some Tips For Your Daily Practice

Pause at the Triveni *(Pre-Coaching Centering Ritual)*

Before you begin a coaching session, take a moment to center yourself at the confluence of the three intelligences. Remember, you are not just a coach; you are the sacred riverbed where transformation flows.

Do this quietly before your next session:

1. Sit still.
2. Place one hand on your head (brain), one on your heart, and one on your belly (gut/soul). Or simply bring attention to these centers.
3. Breathe in deeply.

Whisper inwardly:

- *"Let me create safety."*
- *"Let me feel what needs to be felt."*
- *"Let me see who this person is becoming."*

One breath for each.
Then begin the session, not just from technique, but from alignment.

## Coaching Dialogue Excerpt: The Triveni in Action

Here's a brief fictionalized coaching moment that illustrates how a single session can flow through the three intelligences, creating deep and lasting transformation:

Client: I don't know why I freeze every time I'm about to speak in team meetings.

Coach (softly): Can we pause? What's happening in your body right now?

Client: My chest feels tight. Like I'm holding my breath.

*(The coach guides three grounding breaths -brain/nervous system)*

Coach: If that feeling had a voice, what might it say?

Client: "Don't mess up. They'll judge you."

*(The coach holds space as emotion surfaces - emotional intelligence)*

Coach: And what does the wisest part of you know about this fear?

Client (quietly): That it's old. And I'm not that girl anymore. I have something worth saying.

*(A deeper truth lands- spiritual intelligence)*

Coach: What would it mean to speak and not to prove, but to honor who you've become?

*(The client exhales. A shift has occurred.)*

Insight. Emotion. Meaning. When all three are touched, change becomes inevitable.

The work of truly transformational coaching begins when we learn to see, feel, and honor what is invisible in the client, and in ourselves. What follows is the essence of a mentoring session.

## A reflection on presence, process, and the unseen truths we're called to hold

When I was asked this question by a room full of accomplished coaches;
*"How do we coach the invisible?"*
I paused. Not for an answer, but to feel into the question.
Because the invisible isn't something you explain.
It's something you *listen for*.

You don't begin with action plans. You begin with attunement..

*To begin with, embody a coaching mindset as a way of being.*
You become more than a question-asker. You become a space-holder. A mirror. A vessel.

Your energy signals: *"I will not rush you. I will not fix you. I will walk with you."* This mindset creates safety & trust, and this is the soil in which the invisible begins to speak.

*Then, anchor yourself in Presence.*

Not performance. Not alertness.
A grounded presence. The kind that listens with the whole body.

This is where invisible coaching begins:
in the silence between words,
in the tremor beneath *"I'm fine,"*
in the shift of breath,
in what wasn't said, but was fully felt.

*Only then do you listen deeply and actively*

You're listening to words
You're listening to the story under the story.
You're listening to the client's energetic field,
their belief systems, their emotional patterns,
their unspoken longings.

You're not trying to decode them.
You're allowing their deeper truth to surface; at its own pace.

From there, you begin to evoke awareness

Which may seem like delivering insights.
It's truly about *midwifing realizations.*
Letting the client see what they already sense.
Helping them hear the voice they've quieted for too long.

You stay present as they shift; from autopilot to choice, from narrative to truth.

And only then, do you facilitate growth.

Real growth doesn't come from strategy alone.
It comes when something inside the client moves.
When an outdated identity softens.
When a buried value reclaims its place.
When a long-held belief gives way to a deeper knowing.

*And that's when aligned action naturally emerges.*
Not forced. Not prescribed.
But invited from a more authentic place.

That is the real sequence of coaching.
You don't begin with action.
You begin with listening.
To the noise; to the quiet.
To the obvious; to the invisible.

Until you've seen what's unseen…
you're not really coaching. You're just helping someone rearrange the surface.

But when you coach the invisible
*That's when the real shift happens.*

When we meet the whole human and not just the goals, they open. Wholeness doesn't need fixing, it needs honoring. And when we hold space for what is invisible yet deeply felt, the right interventions arise. These are the moments where coaching shifts from insight to integration, from conversation to transformation. From here, we don't just design interventions that work; we design interventions that *stick*.

## A Wish for You, Dear Reader

May you sit in presence so deep,
that safety is felt without words.
May you listen so openly,
that emotions feel welcomed home.
May you see with soul-eyes,
the truth of who your client is becoming.
And may your interventions not just teach,
but transform.

# Chapter 12: The Future of Coaching: What's Next?

***"If you want to awaken all of humanity, then awaken all of yourself."*** *- Lao Tzu*

## Standing at the Edge of a New Horizon

We are standing at a powerful threshold.

The world is shifting, quickly and profoundly stretching the boundaries of what we know, how we lead, and who we are becoming. Technology is evolving at exponential speed. Workplaces are becoming more complex, more global, and more uncertain. The very definition of success is being rewritten in boardrooms, and in the quiet hearts of individuals longing for purpose, meaning, and a sense of wholeness.

And coaching stands at this intersection, poised not just to respond to the future, but to shape it.

In the early days, coaching was primarily about goal achievement, strategic thinking, and performance enhancement. Today, it is a gateway to inner transformation, a sacred space where awareness unfolds and deeper truths are born. Tomorrow, it will be something even more potent, a catalyst for conscious evolution, helping individuals and systems move from fear to freedom, from confusion to clarity and from separation to unity.

As the world becomes more digitized, more fast-paced, and paradoxically, more disconnected, the need for conscious, human-centered coaching will only grow. Clients will not only ask, "*How do I lead better?*" but also seek deeper truths to align their life and leadership like "*Who am I becoming?*" or "*What impact am I leaving behind?*"

This chapter is an invitation to see what lies ahead, through the traditional lens of strategy and skill, enhanced through the eyes of the soul. Together, we will explore:

- The rise of consciousness-based coaching
- The profound opportunities and ethical tensions that come with artificial intelligence
- What it truly means to evolve as a coach in this age of acceleration

This is about becoming better coaches who are fuller, wiser, more awakened versions of ourselves. Let's dive in!

## The Rise of Consciousness-Based Coaching

### From Performance to Presence

There was a time when coaching was synonymous with productivity. Set a SMART goal. Break it down. Take action. Measure progress. Repeat. This model served its purpose, especially in the early days when coaching emerged from corporate boardrooms and performance psychology.

Then something began to shift.

Coaches started noticing what clients *weren't* saying. The hesitation behind a confident tone, the tightness behind a smile, the dissonance between success and satisfaction. Beneath goals were stories. Beneath stories were emotions. Beneath emotions were identities searching for meaning.

Clients began asking, *"How can I do more?" "Why am I doing it?"* and *"Who am I doing it for?"*

This is where consciousness-based coaching took root. It is a shift from doing to being, from fixing to holding, from performance to presence. Here, the coach is no longer a guide with a map but a mirror, supporting the client as they see themselves not only as a channel for roles and routines, but as a living system of values, beliefs, emotions, and energy.

Presence becomes the most powerful tool. In a world full of noise, offering a silent, attuned space is revolutionary. Conscious coaching is about lasting alignment with perceptible wins. It is about enabling the client to make choices rooted in clarity, courage, and coherence. It is not about driving results at the cost of wholeness.

Remember, in this evolving landscape, clients aren't just seeking answers. They're seeking *themselves.*

## Integrating Spiritual Intelligence and Inner Wisdom

If emotional intelligence (EI) is the ability to recognize, understand, and manage emotions, spiritual intelligence (SQ) is the ability to live with purpose, compassion, and connectedness, a path to lead with wisdom rather than ego.

As coaches, when we help clients access their spiritual intelligence, we invite them to look beyond assigned duties, beyond KPIs and career ladders. We invite them into deeper reflection:

- What does my life want to express through me?
- Where am I being called to grow, to surrender, to evolve?

- What truths have I been avoiding because they don't fit the narrative of success I've built?

In this space, language softens. Insight arises not from thinking harder, but from feeling deeper.

Here, intuition becomes a co-pilot. Stillness becomes a strategy. Clients begin to discover that their deepest wisdom does not lie in logic alone. It lies in the quiet inner voice that just *knows*, without knowing how it knows.

I often refer to the mythical confluence of three rivers in India: the *Ganga* (visible), the *Yamuna* (visible), and the *Saraswati* (invisible). Similarly, coaching at its most potent is the meeting point of three intelligences:

- *Neuroscience* (the structure of thought),
- *Emotional Intelligence* (the energy of feeling), and
- *Spiritual Intelligence* (the silence of knowing)

When we coach from this understanding, we help clients move *inward*, to reconnect with the source of their own truth.

## Coaching the Invisible in a World Obsessed with the Tangible

Modern life is addicted to visibility. Metrics, milestones, dashboards. We are trained to value only what can be seen, measured, and displayed.

But the deepest shifts in coaching are often invisible.

You cannot see a belief unravel.
You cannot track a moment of surrender.
There is no app for a softened heart.

And yet, these are the moments that change everything.

Consciousness-based coaching invites us to trust the unseen. To create space where the client can meet their own vulnerability without shame. To allow silence to speak, rather than rushing to fill it with techniques.

This kind of coaching is about adding more and removing what no longer serves. It is a spiritual decluttering. The role of the coach here is not to advise, analyze, or even "fix". The role of the coach is to *hold space* so that the client can remember who they are beneath the roles they play, beyond the mundane.

In a world that worships speed, we become sacred spaces to slow down.
In a world that seeks answers, we become deep questioners.
In a world that fears uncertainty, we become companions in the unknown.

And that, is the future of coaching
Deeper, truer, and more human than ever before.

## AI and Technology in Coaching: Friend or Foe?

AI is here to stay. And it's an important fillip to the coaching business. Yes, there are legitimate fears that a lot of coaching work will be transferred to specialized GPTs or something similar. In my opinion, it's a very welcome opportunity to up the coaching game.

How?

Well, adopters will start working on higher order coaching – including identity, spirituality, social and emotional intelligence, in addition to higher order attitudinal drivers such as values. Simply stated, coaching in the age of AI will more decisively gravitate towards the invisible aspects of the whole person. This might be more rewarding and fulfilling work than we have ever done before.

Non- or late adopters are likely to be increasingly challenged to coach as they know it today. They may be forced into the same, or a lower level, than the one AI based coaching will serve. This could include creating their own GPTs, incident coaching, templatizing, monetizing social media and other opportunities that may arise at the lower end of the pyramid.

Neither model is right or wrong. It's a matter of choice, and a forecast that Artificial Intelligence WILL move your cheese. As a coach, you're going to find out where the cheese moved, and gravitate in the direction of your choice.

This new disruption in coaching will probably replace the bulk of what Coaching constitutes today, which is the visible. These are mostly behavioral and performance related coaching. Clients will increasingly gravitate towards AI for performance, behavior and skills-based coaching.

Viewed in the context of Pareto's principle, while 80% of issues coached today are behavioral and only 20% are non-behavioral, invisible ones, AI will increasingly force the ratio to be reversed."

**The Age of Intelligent Assistance**

The digital revolution has seeped into every aspect of our lives and coaching is no exception.

Today, coaches have access to sophisticated platforms that can transcribe sessions in real-time, analyze vocal tones for emotional insight, and track language patterns to identify limiting beliefs. AI tools can support scheduling, automate session follow-ups, and even generate reflective prompts based on a client's narrative.

On the surface, these tools seem to promise the golden trifecta: efficiency, consistency, and scale. Imagine coaching a client with the support of an AI assistant who reminds you of recurring metaphors from six sessions ago or flags a sudden emotional shift in tone you may have missed. It feels like augmentation, not replacement.

In fact, for many coaches, especially those running practices across geographies, AI can feel like a welcome ally, a backstage support system that lets them focus more fully on presence.

And yet, this raises an urgent question:

*"At what point does the line blur between assistance and replacement?"*

**What AI Can't Do, And Must Never Replace**

Coaching is a profession where the foundation lies in a profoundly human encounter.

AI can simulate empathy. It can mimic active listening. It can even be trained to ask powerful questions based on language models. But it cannot *feel.* It cannot be moved by a client's pain. It cannot hold the energy of grief, joy, shame, or hope in the sacred silence between words.

A coach's presence is not data. It is the aliveness in the room. The micro-expressions. The subtle intuition that nudges a coach to ask a question they hadn't planned. The stillness that allows a client to cry, not as a result of the coach doing anything, but truly because the coach did not fill the space.

Coaching is a dance. It is a resonance of nervous systems, a sacred witnessing of the human journey. AI can't replicate these aspects because these cannot be reduced to code.

There is also a deeper ethical concern: data privacy and trust. Clients share their rawest truths with us. Do we fully understand how their data is being stored, used, or processed by the tools we employ? If we don't, we are unconsciously breaching the sanctity of coaching.

So, as we integrate technology, we must remember that the essence of coaching lies in presence, not in processing.

However, the dilemma continues!

To resist technology entirely is to become obsolete. To surrender to it blindly is to lose the soul of our craft.

The path lies in *co-evolving* with technology, where we integrate with discernment.

Yes, we can use AI to support session summaries or identify linguistic patterns. To uphold an ethical practice, we must remain the ones interpreting the nuance. We can use dashboards to notice trends, but we must continue to trust our intuition. We can partner with apps that track emotional states, but we must remain the ones who hold emotional safety.

More than ever, coaches will be called to evolve their own presence to become so deeply attuned, so fully grounded, that no machine can replicate their being.

What this means practically:

- Mastery in *presence* becomes more valuable than mastery in frameworks.
- Emotional and spiritual intelligence become competitive advantages in a world where cognitive skill is increasingly automated.
- Coaches must become educators, helping clients understand the ethical implications of tech, guiding them toward conscious digital choices.

Just as technology evolves, so must we.
Not to compete, but to co-create a future where technology serves humanity, not the other way around.

This is not just a professional imperative.
It is a *spiritual calling.*

## The Evolving Coach: A Journey of Mastery and Meaning

### From Technician to Transformation Catalyst

The early coach was often seen as a technician; a skilled facilitator who could ask powerful questions, guide action plans, and create accountability. Competence was measured by how well one followed models and frameworks.

But the clients of tomorrow don't just want support.
They want an *awakening.*
They want to be seen, not just assessed.
They want to be challenged, not just encouraged.
They want to be met at the depth of their being.

This calls for a new archetype of the coach: as a facilitator of performance, and a *catalyst for transformation.* Someone who can walk with the client into the shadows, sit with silence, and call forth the brilliance buried under years of conditioning.

In this new paradigm, technique alone is not enough.
The coach must embody *wisdom.*

However, Wisdom is not accumulated knowledge.
It is the capacity to be fully present with not knowing.
It is the humility to hold paradoxes without needing to solve them.
It is the grace to sense when to step in and when to simply hold space.

As the outer world becomes increasingly complex, clients will seek coaches who have done their inner work; who can hold ambiguity without collapsing, who can embody stillness amidst urgency, and who can listen with their whole being.

Becoming that kind of coach is not a certification.
It is a commitment.

## Continuous Learning in the Age of Acceleration

In a world where new technologies and ideas emerge almost weekly, standing still is not an option. Coaches must evolve to stay relevant, but to stay resonant. Learning today is not about attending another training or collecting more hours. It is about deeper integration. Ask yourself:

- What am I practicing? Not just in my sessions, but in my life?
- Where am I triggered, and what does that reveal about my shadow self?
- How deeply do I listen, to others, and to myself?

With the current trends in new tools and technology, it is imperative that the coach of the future is a lifelong learner who has the ability to unlearn as well. They have to be willing to let go of tools that no longer serve them. Willing to be undone by new perspectives. Willing to stay open, humble, and curious.

Peer supervision, reflective journaling, mindfulness practices, and dialogue circles will become more important than ever. These are not add-ons; they are anchors.

In the age of acceleration, the greatest gift a coach can offer is *slowness.*

Slowness not in pace, but slowness in presence.
The kind of presence that only comes from deep inner clarity.

## Developing Meta-Competence

The ICF Core Competencies have served as a foundational framework for coaches across the globe. They define key behaviors that promote effectiveness, ethics, and presence.

In the coaching spaces of tomorrow, we will need to go a level deeper than some of the current frameworks and competencies offer. Not to discard these competencies, but to transcend them. To move from skill to *meta-skill.* From *technique* to *awareness.*

Meta-competence is the ability to coach from the whole self. It is the capacity to stay attuned to multiple layers at once:

- The spoken and the unspoken
- The individual and the systemic
- The client's words and their energy
- The present moment and the emerging future

It's being aware of our own biases in real-time, without letting them distort the field. It's noticing our own emotional landscape while remaining fully attuned to the client's. It's sensing the field–not just the individual.

This level of mastery is not performative. It is *embodied.*
It cannot be faked. It must be lived.

And this is perhaps the most urgent evolution the coaching profession must embrace: to move beyond what we do, and deeply into who we are.

Because in the end, the client is not transformed by our frameworks. They are transformed by our presence.

## Case Study: Coaching in the Age of AI

*Client Profile:*

Name: Jen
Role: Global Vice President – Product Innovation
Industry: Artificial Intelligence and Ethics
Location: APAC HQ
Organization: A multinational tech conglomerate known for pioneering AI applications across education, healthcare, and defense.

### The Coaching Mandate: Leading with Soul in a System of Speed

When Jen approached me for coaching, she was already seen as a visionary. She was responsible for launching several AI products that were transforming how knowledge was accessed and distributed. Internally, she was celebrated for her strategic mind and her ability to deliver complex projects across timelines most considered impossible.

And yet, something in her voice told a different story.

She was increasingly uncomfortable with the pace of decisions, the ethical grey zones in AI deployment, and the gradual erosion of human judgment in favor of machine logic. She wasn't burnt out in the traditional sense; she was spiritually exhausted. Disconnected from her own values, unsure whether the future she was helping shape was one she wanted to live in.

"*I feel like I'm feeding a beast I no longer believe in,*" she said in one of our early sessions.

This was not a request for performance coaching.
*It was a cry for reconnection.*

**The Coaching Approach: Consciousness-Based and Systemic**

Our coaching journey was designed to help Jen "perform better," and to help her lead more consciously with alignment, discernment, and courage.

We worked across three layers:

1. The Inner Landscape: Realigning Values and Voice

- We began with a series of deep reflective inquiries:
    - What is the deeper intelligence guiding my leadership?
    - Where have I outsourced my inner compass to external metrics?
    - How do I define integrity in an age where speed outruns ethics?
- Through guided visualizations, journaling, and embodied presence practices, Jen began to reconnect with a part of

herself she had long silenced: the wise observer. The part that knew when something felt "*off*" even if the data said otherwise.
- Her emotional vocabulary expanded. She moved from intellectual explanations to heartfelt truths. Coaching helped her reclaim her inner authority.

2. The Relational Field: Leading Ethically in a Hyper-Productive System

- Jen realized that her leadership style had become reactive. She was mirroring the system's speed instead of shaping it.
- We explored how to slow down the pace of conversations, bring mindfulness into decision-making, and normalize ethical pause in meetings.
- She piloted a "Tech + Ethics Forum" within her division, bringing together engineers, ethicists, and product managers for reflective dialogue before high-impact launches.

3. The Systemic Impact: Coaching the Future Through the Present

- One of the most powerful shifts happened when Jen began viewing her role not just as a VP, but as a custodian of future consciousness.
- She asked bold questions in executive reviews. *"Is it scalable?,"* of course, but more importantly– *"is it soul-aligned?"*
- Her influence began to ripple. Other leaders started inquiring about coaching. Product teams asked for value-alignment workshops. The culture began to shift; subtly but surely.

## The Outcome: A New Kind of Leadership Presence

Jen didn't leave her role. She reclaimed it, with clarity, compassion, and courage.

She reported feeling more centered, more honest, and more empowered to say no when something felt misaligned. She integrated mindfulness into her team's rituals and introduced spiritual intelligence as a leadership capacity, not as religion, but as the wisdom to act with humility, interdependence, and heart.

Her team launched a new AI-powered product six months later with embedded ethical nudges, transparency features, and optional human override built in.

This wasn't just a technical feature.
It was a reflection of her inner transformation.

"*I learned that the world doesn't need more brilliant minds disconnected from their souls,*" she told me at the end of our journey. "*It needs leaders who are awake to their power, their impact, and their responsibility.*"

## A Call to the Future: Becoming the Coaches the World Needs

We are not just coaches.
We are stewards of consciousness.
We are catalysts to a new kind of leadership, a new way of being.

The future *will* be defined by those who are present, who evolve. The clients of tomorrow will not be satisfied with superficial goals. They will seek alignment, depth, and awakening. They will come with questions the mind cannot answer but the heart can hold. And it is up to us as coaches, mentors, educators to rise to this call.

We are being invited to evolve through being our authentic selves; vulnerable, adaptable, grounded, awake, and deeply human.

### The Coach as Lighthouse

In stormy waters, ships don't look for faster engines.
They look for *light*.

The coach of the future is a lighthouse; they know how to stand still, anchored in presence, offering clarity without control.

They listen.to words, to energy.
They see behavior patterns.
They speak to evoke the voice, the essence that is waiting to be heard.

They are not distracted by performance.
They are attuned to purpose.

**Coaching as a Sacred Responsibility**

In this age of AI, virtual connection, and global acceleration, it becomes even more essential that coaching does not lose its *soul.*

Let technology enhance your reach.
Let neuroscience enrich your insight.
Let spiritual intelligence guide your presence.

But let your *humanity* remain at the center.

Your ability to hold space; courage to reflect the unseen. Your willingness to stay with discomfort; trust in silence. Your love for the truth, no matter how inconvenient it may be.

This is the real edge of coaching.

**Three Reflections for the Road Ahead**

As you continue your journey, I invite you to sit with these questions, and ponder the direction of your practice:

1. What kind of coach do I need to become to meet the needs of tomorrow?
   Not just in skill, but in presence, ethics, and depth.
2. How can I preserve the human soul of coaching while integrating technology with discernment?
   Not resisting progress, but guiding it from a place of wisdom.

3. Am I willing to be changed by the very transformation I invite in others?
   Not just teaching growth, but embodying it.

The future of coaching is not external or out there somewhere. It is unfolding within us.

With every session we hold, with every silence we honor, with every breakthrough we witness, we are shaping the coaching profession for today's leaders, and for generations to come.

And perhaps that is the deepest purpose of all to coach for outcomes, through awakening. To be quiet revolutionaries. To be vessels of clarity in a time of confusion. To be sacred spaces in a world that has forgotten how to pause.

We are not just shaping conversations.
We are shaping consciousness.

Let us do it with courage. With presence. And with love.

## Reflection: Ethical Considerations in AI-Enhanced Coaching

### AI in Coaching: 5 Ethical Questions Every Coach Must Ask

As AI becomes more integrated into coaching systems, we must remain vigilant. Here are five critical reflections:

1. Informed Consent
   Have I clearly informed the client when AI tools are being used to record, transcribe, or analyze our sessions?

2. Data Ownership
   Who owns the data generated by the session? Where is it stored, and for how long?

3. Bias in Algorithms
   Are the AI tools I'm using built on inclusive, bias-checked datasets? Or do they reflect dominant worldviews?

4. Client Autonomy
   Does the client have the right to opt out of any AI-related augmentation? Is their sovereignty preserved?

5. Coaching Essence
   Am I relying on AI insights to replace human presence, or am I using them to deepen it?

Coaching is sacred. Technology must serve that sacredness; not dilute it.

## Practice Guide: Becoming the Coach the Future Needs

### Daily and Weekly Rituals to Deepen Presence, Integrity, and Mastery

| Practice | Frequency | Why It Matters |
|---|---|---|
| Presence Ritual | Daily | Begin your day with breathwork, mindfulness, or stillness to center yourself before holding space for others. |
| Intuitive Debrief | 2–3x/week | After select sessions, reflect: What did I sense beyond the spoken? How did intuition guide the moment? |
| Ethical Reflection Circle | Monthly | Gather with peers or a mentor to explore ethical dilemmas, especially around power, consent, and technology. |
| Coaching Tech Audit | Quarterly | Review tools you're using: are they aligned with your values? Are they enhancing or interfering with presence |
| Spiritual Integration Practice | Weekly | Use journaling, nature walks, or silent contemplation to stay aligned with your inner compass and deeper purpose. |
| Mentor Supervision or Peer Dialogue | Ongoing | Coaching the future requires evolving with others. Regular dialogue sharpens both skill and soul. |

The coaches of tomorrow are not only better trained. They are more attuned.

Let your *daily rhythm* reflect the depth you seek to hold for others.

# Conclusion: Coaching for Deeper Impact

## The Journey Inward – Revisited

We began this book with a simple question: *What truly drives transformation in coaching?* Not just temporary performance shifts or surface-level goals, but deep, sustained change that shapes identity, relationships, and legacy.

Throughout these chapters, we explored the invisible forces that underpin every coaching conversation—emotions, beliefs, values, intuitive nudges, and spiritual stirrings. We ventured beyond conventional goal-setting frameworks and into the terrain of human consciousness. From emotional mastery to inner wisdom, from presence to spiritual intelligence, each chapter built on the premise that *what is unseen often holds the greatest power.*

This is the new frontier of coaching: not just as a practice to improve performance, but as a profound catalyst for transformation.

## Coaching as a Force for Change

The ripple effects of this kind of coaching are immeasurable.

When one leader learns to navigate conflict with emotional awareness, it changes a team.

When a founder reconnects with purpose, it alters the trajectory of an organization.

When an individual heals inner wounds and shows up whole, it impacts families, communities, and generations.

Coaching, when done at depth, becomes a social force. It moves beyond individual goals and enters the realm of collective evolution.

And that is our invitation to see ourselves not just as service providers or accountability partners, but as co-stewards in humanity's awakening.

The world doesn't need more productivity hacks. It needs more emotionally wise, spiritually anchored, and neurologically attuned humans. That is the work. And it begins with us.

Is Real time Coaching on Human Behavior in Organizations missing in the Corporate world.?

*Human Behavior in an Organization should be driven by the 'Values' practiced by an Organization.*

*Very rarely do Managers receive coaching to understand Human Behavior which can help them build trust, communicate effectively, make fair decisions, and create inclusive, psychologically productive work environments. They are well trained to respond to data, but not to emotions, motivations, and interpersonal dynamics—which ultimately leads to better team performance, innovation, and long-term organizational success. If this Coaching is done by the Boss, It enhances the EQ of the Manager, which helps in the Journey of Good to Great Managers.*

*There is clearly a role for Coaching young Managers on Human Behavior by their Supervisor. Coaching in Corporates is definitely required on this invisible part. Good Supervisor and Good Coaches need to identify gaps on IQ:EQ Coefficient.*

*- Venky Venkatesh, Former CEO, Press Trust of India; experienced Business Leader at Hindustan Unilever & HT Media*

## Bringing the Invisible into Practice

So, what now?

You've explored the philosophies, the models, the case studies, and the metaphors. But transformation doesn't happen in reading alone. It happens in reflection, application, and embodiment.

As you close this book, I invite you to pause to reflect on what you've learned, and to tune in to who you're becoming.

Coaching is not something you perform; it's something you become. With every session, you shape not only your client's future but your own.

Let the wisdom of these three intelligences ripple through your presence, your words, and your listening. Let your coaching impact individuals to elevate humanity.

Some suggestions for the journey forward:

**1. Commit to Your Own Inner Work**

A coach can only take the client as far as they've gone themselves. So ask:

- What emotions do you still avoid?
- What unconscious patterns influence your coaching?
- Where do you still operate from ego or fear?

The more self-aware you are, the more invisible threads you can sense in your clients.

**2. Weave the Three Intelligences into Your Coaching**

- Begin your sessions with emotional check-ins, not agendas.
- Use neuroscience insights to explain habits, triggers, and rewiring.
- Invite clients to explore their deeper "why," inner wisdom, or soulful longings.

Even subtle integrations of EQ, neuroscience, and SQ can dramatically shift outcomes.

### 3. Develop Practices for Presence and Intuition

Stillness is a skill. So is intuitive listening.
Experiment with mindfulness, reflective journaling, or body-based practices that enhance your perceptive field.

Presence isn't just about being in the moment; it's about *becoming a clear vessel for insight to emerge.*

### 4. Hold Space for the Invisible

Don't rush to fix.
Don't fill every silence.
Don't always offer the clever question.

Sometimes the deepest shifts happen when the coach simply holds space with reverence, with trust, and with a deep respect for the client's inner knowing.

### 5. Lead with Heart and Humility

The more tools we gain, the more we must remember: *We are not the change-makers. The client is.*

Our job is to hold the mirror, shine the light, and trust the process

The evolved coach is not defined by tools or techniques alone, but by the presence they embody. They are emotionally wise, grounded in self-awareness, empathy, and the capacity to hold space for the full spectrum of human emotion. They are neuroscience-aware, understanding the brain's wiring, working with habit loops, and facilitating sustainable behavioral shifts. At their core, they are spiritually anchored, tuned into a deeper sense of purpose, intuition, and the unseen layers of consciousness that guide transformation. They remain deeply present, centered and unhurried, fully attuned to the moment and what is emerging within it. They are intuitively responsive, trusting silence, inner knowing, and the wisdom that arises between the words. Above all, the evolved coach becomes a mirror and a channel—not one who solves or advises, but one who reveals, reflects, and awakens.

This is not a final destination.
It is a continuous practice.
A way of being.

Before you move on to your next client or session, take a moment to pause.

Ask yourself:

- *What invisible shift has occurred in me while reading this book?*
- *How will I now show up differently—in coaching, and in life?*
- *What part of my own consciousness am I being called to evolve next?*

Closing Thoughts…

In the stillness of twilight, a single lamp is lit.
Its flame flickers gently, steady and warm.
As another approaches, the flame extends

Not dimming, but multiplying.
Light passes from wick to wick.
No words spoken. Just presence shared.

This is the essence of coaching.
To be the lamp that lights another—
Not by force, but by being fully lit from within.

When your light is steady, others find their way.
And in that quiet glow, transformation takes root.

## An Invitation to the Movement

If this book stirred something within you; an insight, a calling, a quiet whisper- you are not alone.

There is a growing community of coaches who are choosing to work not just from skill, but from soul. Coaches who are committed to deep presence, emotional clarity, and spiritual grounding. Coaches who see their role not as fixing, but as facilitating human evolution.

If you feel called to explore this path further
To deepen your practice,
To connect with fellow travelers,
To bring neuroscience, EQ, and SQ into your coaching with grace and mastery

You are warmly invited to be part of this unfolding movement. Write to me at sandhyamathur@inwardfocus.in for a free consult.

The journey inward is not meant to be walked alone.

Thank you for walking this path with me.
— *Sandhya*

# More Praise for the Book

Through lived experiences of being coached or mentored with the methodology written about.

- *Unified Endorsement for Coaches – Expanding the Horizon*

"*Coaching the Invisible* is not just a book, it's an invitation to evolve. As a coach, a leader, and founder of E1Global, a movement centered on developing the mind, body, and soul, I've seen firsthand how coaching often stays confined to frameworks, checklists, and outcomes. Sandhya Mathur opens a powerful door to what lies beyond.

This work is a profound reminder that transformation doesn't begin with action, it begins with presence. Mathur masterfully bridges emotional intelligence, neuroscience, and spiritual insight, guiding coaches into the deeper, often unseen dimensions of human growth. She gives voice to what many of us have felt intuitively: that true coaching means honoring the whole person—not just their goals, but their grief, their values, their yearning for meaning.

For coaches ready to move beyond the surface; for those who know there's more to this craft than behavior change; this book is both a roadmap and a companion. It will sharpen your skills, expand your presence, and ultimately, shift how you coach, lead, and live.

Read it slowly. Return to it often. Let it rewire how you see yourself and those you serve.

*For the Whole Human*

"As someone who believes in training the whole person: Mind, Body, and Soul, I found Coaching the Invisible to be both a validation and a revelation. Sandhya Mathur doesn't just teach coaching, she restores its original purpose: to guide humans through meaningful inner change. In a field increasingly focused on performance metrics, this book reminds us that sustainable impact comes from coaching the unseen forces—identity, values, and emotion. Whether you're a coach, leader, or warrior for human potential, this book will elevate your approach and your outcomes."

- *Gabriel M. Menchaca, U.S. Special Agent (Retired)*

"As a fellow coach and someone who deeply respects Sandhya Mathur and her work, I was immediately drawn to the depth and clarity of Coaching the Invisible. The focus on the unseen dimensions of coaching—inner narratives, emotional undercurrents, and quiet shifts—is where true transformation begins. This book offers something rare: a grounded, intuitive approach that speaks directly to what matters most in our work. I truly believe this work has the potential to transform how coaches show up—and how clients experience growth."

- *Rezina Denis Coach | Author | Human Capital Practitioner*

"This book is both deeply personal and powerfully practical. As someone fortunate to have been mentored by Sandhya Mathur, I can say with complete honesty: her insights have changed the trajectory of my coaching and leadership journey. What she brings together—neuroscience, emotional and spiritual intelligence, mentorship, and transformational coaching—has helped me grow not only as a professional, but as a person.

Whether you're an experienced coach or stepping into leadership for the first time, this book will stretch you, ground you, and equip you to lead with greater clarity, presence, and purpose. I've felt the impact firsthand—and I believe anyone who engages with this work will too."

- *Lisa Bishop Leadership Development Consultant & Executive Coach The Bishop Concept*

"It's a rare privilege to learn from someone who not only imparts knowledge but also catalyzes true transformation. Sandhya Mathur, (author of this book) has been that kind of mentor in my life—guiding me with depth, clarity, and compassion on my journey as a coach and leader.

What she offers in these pages is far more than a framework; it's an invitation to lead from a place of inner alignment and elevated awareness. This book integrates neuroscience, emotional and cognitive intelligence, spiritual insight, and the often-underestimated power of mentorship into a roadmap for sustainable personal and professional growth.

As a coach and leader, I've already begun to experience how her teachings have reshaped the way I show up, for myself, for others, and for the systems I serve. Her approach goes beneath surface-level strategies and into the real work: expanding consciousness, developing presence, and leading with intention.

For anyone seeking to evolve, whether as a coach, a leader, or a human being; this book will serve as a companion, a mirror, and a guide. It has already impacted me profoundly, and I know it will do the same for many others.

As my mentor coach, Sandhya didn't just sharpen my skills—she helped me deepen my coaching presence. This book reflects that gift: grounded in science, infused with spiritual insight, and rich with wisdom for any coach ready to evolve beyond traditional technique. It's not just a read—it's a fresh lens into what truly creates transformation. This will be a trusted companion and a living resource in your coaching practice for decades to come."

- *Cecil Hudson, Founder, Coaching & Development Insights*

"*Coaching the Invisible*" is as luminous as Sandhya herself.

To me, Sandhya is like a chandelier; she doesn't just light up a space; she lifts it. Whether in coaching sessions, one-to-one conversations, or while nurturing others, her presence is both functional and beautiful, a true anchor of grace and depth.

My favorite part is her story of evolution as a coach; moving from trying to adapt, following processes, and applying models to shining in her own signature style. It's a style that blends neuroscience, emotional intelligence (EQ), and spiritual intelligence (SQ) into a soulful, transformational practice.

As a reader, if you are a rising coach like me, you'll gain a deeper language of influence that speaks to what's unspoken. If you are a coach practitioner in the journey of mastery, you'll deepen emotional mastery and discover practical models that shift mindset and identity. If you are a leader in self-discovery, you'll learn to integrate IQ, EQ, and SQ to lead with clarity, purpose, and presence. This book will not just grow your toolkit—it will grow you.

This book feels like a warm conversation with Sandhya—quietly powerful and deeply illuminating. It's not just a guide; it's a light.

- *Debeshi Chakraborty, PCC*

Sandhya Mathur has masterfully distilled her thousands of hours of coaching experience and profound insights into this remarkable book, making it an engaging and transformative read. Her use of rich and varied metaphors is especially powerful, leaving a lasting imprint of the learnings and wisdom she shares. This is truly a one-of-a-kind work that uniquely weaves together spirituality, neuroscience, emotional intelligence, and the science of coaching. I wholeheartedly recommend this book to every life coach—whether new or seasoned—who aspires to elevate their practice and excel in deep, impactful coaching."

- *Baskaran Rajamani PCC, Retired Partner, Deloitte. Canada and Seasoned Executive Coach*

"Sandhya Mathur has been a guiding force in both the coaching industry and the leadership realm. Her approach to coaching has left a lasting impact on how coaches and leaders support others. In a world where performance often overshadows people, this book is a timely and essential reminder that effective leadership begins with truly seeing and understanding the individual & not just the goal. If you're looking to bring more humanity into your conversations, this book offers insight, wisdom, and the voice of someone who genuinely walks the talk.

- *Afsheen Dattoobhai PCC, Creative Life & Executive Coach, Mentor coach*